Against All Odds

Also published by and available from

Merlin Unwin Books
7 Corve Street, Ludlow
Shropshire SY8 1DB.

Orderline: 01584 877456

LONDON POLICE: their stories (£7.99)
ROUGH JUSTICE: memoirs of a Flying Squad detective (£7.99)

Against All Odds

The Remarkable Adventures of PC Jim Beard

by ex-PC Jim Beard

MERLIN UNWIN BOOKS

First published in Great Britain by Merlin Unwin Books, 2001

Published by

Merlin Unwin Books
Palmers House
7 Corve Street
Ludlow
Shropshire SY8 1DB
U. K.

A CIP catalogue record for this book is available from the British Library

ISBN 1–873674–50-3

Designed and produced by Merlin Unwin Books, Ludlow
Jacket design: Mary Hayter
Printed in Great Britain by Bell & Bain Ltd, Glasgow

Contents

Introduction

For the past 50 years, I have always kept a diary of the events that have happened to me, some amusing, some tragic.

People have often suggested that I write a book about my experiences. Well, I have now decided that I would like to share my experiences with others, including of course my old colleagues, young policemen and even my old Guvnors.

You are now holding in your hands my memoirs of all those years. I hope you enjoy reading this book as much as I have enjoyed recalling these stories for you.

What am I doing now, you may ask. Well, I enjoy meeting and corresponding with my old buddies, like Detective Chief Superintendent Mike O'Leary, and when we get together we reminisce for hours on end. Mike and I also talk about the days of the British Airways fraud, recorded in this book. He has had a number of heart attacks in recent years, as well as a heart by-pass operation. Sadly for me, he has moved to New Zealand with his family so I don't get to see him any more.

Another close friend of mine is Detective Chief Inspector Hugh Parker (no relation to Hughie of Mill Hill) who runs his own detective agency in Ashtead, Surrey, and he calls in to see me now and again; or if he can't get to see me, he gives me a ring and we have long chats on the telephone. Hughie has a villa in Spain, about 40 miles north of Benidorm. It is a wonderful place to stay in and it is even recommended by the World Health Organisation, which is good enough for me.

I remember one day telling Hugh that I'd forgotten to get my wife a birthday present. Unfortunately, it was too late to go to the shops. Hugh told me not to worry and said, 'For ten shillings I have here a bottle of scent.' I knew his wife sold scent and so I went ahead and purchased it. He also gave me a lovely presentation box, which showed off the bottle beautifully.

Later that evening I made my way home and proudly gave this lovely looking gift to my wife. She opened the case and was extremely happy until she opened the top of the bottle and sniffed at the contents. (It might as well have said light the blue touch paper and run like hell!) She took a nose full of the ghastly stuff and as I ran away the bottle came flying after me. I wasn't allowed to return until the nasty smell had died away; it was possible that the genie had died in the bottle. My wife eventually forgave me when I wined and dined her the following evening to make up for my terrible gift. Hughie and I often laugh about this when we meet. It is incredible to think that it happened over 35 years ago – and it was nearly 30 years before Hughie could face my wife.

This reminded me of another friend who brought a roulette wheel into the police station and said, 'This would be great to raise money for charity.' During the evening he got it working and after finding enough lads to take part he started up the wheel. He asked if he could be the banker - he knew the banker couldn't lose. We all bought some chips. bets were placed and the ball was sent spinning round. He lost - so much for 'the banker can't lose'. Round the ball went again and he lost a second time. On the third round he lost again and kept losing until he had to stop because he had exhausted all his reserves. I turned to him and said, 'The charities will be pleased, so long as they are not the bankers.' We nearly died laughing but we didn't let him go home without giving him his money back. He certainly learned a lesson that day.

I correspond now and then with all the gang of charity organisers, who are all retired of course. There was Norman Wells, Spencer Bell, Ken Moxley, Roger Baxter and Arthur Callaby. We meet at the police reunions, which are held at the Police Club with other officers from all over the United Kingdom. I mustn't forget our Chief Inspector John Roddy who gave us the time to carry out our charity work. When we all meet, you never fail to hear the words, 'Can you remember when...?' Often our wives stop us telling too many stories because they've heard them all before.

I attended the last Gerald Road Police Station Reunion the day it was finally closed in 1995. Hundreds of ex-officers attended the Reunion and it was a very sad occasion. The station has recently been pulled down after 148 years, which is very sad because it was an integral part of Belgravia. The streets were closed to traffic that day and all the local residents joined in the fun. After a final drink with my old mates, I was taken to the nearby railway station and put on a train to Horsham. When I arrived at Horsham I got a taxi home as I was very tired and my legs were giving way. I was so sad to leave the past behind.

The taxi dropped me at the door and I was soon in bed dreaming of times gone by and thinking of all the friends I had made during my long years of service. Then I thought: at least there are no more calls demanding my presence at the nick. I hit the pillow and slept like a log.

I still think about criminals and crime. Much of the work we carried out was very tedious but it was always essential to pay attention to the minor details when bringing a case to trial. I managed to keep cheerful, knowing that the next day would bring new surprises. And it always did, as you will read.

God bless all you serving and ex-coppers.

Jim Beard
August 2001

Acknowledgements

My thanks are due to a great many people:

To my daughter-in-law, Valerie Beard, for writing out the story, in between running her home and job and for getting it all done on time; also to her and her husband (my son), Malcolm Beard, for helping with the proofs and with the Introduction.

To my wife and two sons, Malcolm and Russell Beard, for putting up with me during my hard times, especially for visiting me every day in hospital for the $3^1/2$ years, and for their assistance in reminding me of some of the stories I had told and forgotten over the years!

To John Dorking, my old Inspector from Gerald Road, who painstakingly re-wrote the stories, which took many weeks. He also rectified some of the legal aspects – and asked for no reward.

To Air Marshal Sir Ivor Broom KCB, CBE, DSO, DFC, AFC, a true friend who gave me a good start in life with my education which eventually lead to my joining the Police Force.

To Detective Chief Superintendent Mike O'Leary for his invaluable assistance whilst in the Police Force.

To my dear friend, the BBC journalist Justin Bones.

To Detective Chief Inspector Hugh Parker for reminding me of some of the stories.

To Karen, Tina and staff for their invaluable assistance and time spent putting the book in order, publishing it and distributing it.

To the Police Force in general for giving me many years of pleasure whilst I served at Gerald Road, Chelsea, Cannon Row, Hendon, West Hendon, Mill Hill, Golders Green, Boreham Wood and on the Burglary Squad and all the Murder Squads.

To all the Police Officers known and unknown who still give me laughs in my times of pain, who made this book possible, they were and still are, better than any medicine.

To all the doctors, especially Dr Jarvis, Dr Jones and Dr Kerwin who, with all the nurses, physiotherapists and staff after $3^1/_2$ years got me back on my feet, disabled but now able to walk.

To you the readers who through the purchase of this book have helped me raise money for our police charity, the Police Pensioners' Housing Association. I thank you all from the bottom of my heart.

To anyone I've missed!

Jim Beard
Chelmsford, Essex

Police Pensioners' Housing Association

All profits from sales of this book will go to the Police Pensioners' Housing Association (PPHA), a national charity which provides sheltered housing for retired policemen and policewomen and their spouses. The PPHA has raised thousands of pounds over the years, entirely through an immense amount of selfless, unpaid work by its volunteers and fund-raisers.

Chapter One

THE BEGINNING OF THE END

It was nearly midnight on 28 November 1978. I was driving the police car round my section (all 15 miles of it, including parts of Hertfordshire) when, at the junction of Edgware Road and Stanmore, I saw a car standing in a garage forecourt with the bonnet up and the battery on the ground. I also noticed a lad running along the Edgware Road. As I drove slowly past, I saw two or three figures inside the garage moving about. Suspicious, I reversed at speed, stopped and jumped out of the car. Two men ran out of the garage office, one turning to the left and the other to the right.

I knew the area well and realised I had no hope of catching the lad who had gone to the right. I also knew that the one who went to the left, round the back of the garage, had a 12-foot perimeter fence to climb, so I knew I could catch him.

I ran round to the back of the garage and saw him jump onto the cars, then leap onto the perimeter fence. I did likewise and grabbed him, pulling him back to earth. I had a good grip on him but, unknown to me, his mate had followed me. He came up behind me and – smack – hit me across the back. I heard a loud 'crack' and collapsed to the ground, felled like an ox. The pain was tremendous – I had never felt anything like it. I could not move; I was paralysed. He had hit me with an iron crowbar.

I found myself lying on my back in a puddle and the air temperature was so low that the water was turning to ice underneath me. I was drifting in and out of consciousness but I remembered shouting over my personal radio to my best mate Mick Jones, 'Urgent assistance, Mick,' and heard him reply after a time asking for my whereabouts. By now, both my arms had given out and I couldn't radio him back. I also realised that I could no longer speak. God I was in a state!

My back was hurting like hell, my legs were numb, the use had gone from my arms and the water was freezing my uniform. I was in shock and shivering from the cold and, even if I could have moved, I dared not because I knew one could die from a back injury.

As I lay there, my life passed before me: my childhood, my days rebelling against education, the R.A.F, marriage, my family... Oh Lord, my family! Yes, it is true, your life does pass before you in hopeless situations like mine.

Suddenly the radio crackled and I heard shouts of 'What's your position?' I could also hear calls coming from the Information Room at Scotland Yard on my nearby car radio. They had become involved and were moving a search party into my area from other Stations to look for me, which seemed to be a hopeless task because I was lying flat on my back, hidden behind this bloody garage!

I guessed I had been there for over an hour, because the water was now frozen solid to my coat. It had soaked through my clothes and I understood what it really meant to be 'soaked to the skin'. I was freezing cold and in a hopeless mess. I wondered if I could last much longer. I felt I couldn't last another hour, but I was wrong.

Desperate to remain conscious, I tried to focus on my family, my wife and two boys. What would they all do without me? Recalling when the children had been born and how close we all were brought tears to my eyes.

The searchers were out in force as I heard the messages passing to and fro in the areas they were covering: fields, trees, woods, nothing was overlooked in their efforts to find their missing colleague.

It was now extremely cold. I was wet and I realised my body temperature was well below normal. My condition was getting worse by the minute; even if they found my car they might not find me for ages. Surely someone would come soon. It was an enormous task, with such a wide area to search. I could be anywhere.

Suddenly I heard a man talking to his dog. He was probably taking it for a walk. I tried in vain to shout or even moan so that he could hear me but he walked on, out of earshot, leaving me in an even worse state of hopelessness and desperation. I could only pray that someone might find me soon.

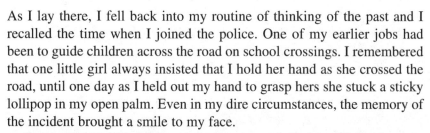

As I lay there, I fell back into my routine of thinking of the past and I recalled the time when I joined the police. One of my earlier jobs had been to guide children across the road on school crossings. I remembered that one little girl always insisted that I hold her hand as she crossed the road, until one day as I held out my hand to grasp hers she stuck a sticky lollipop in my open palm. Even in my dire circumstances, the memory of the incident brought a smile to my face.

I struggled to find another early memory to keep myself slipping into unconsciousness. On another occasion, I was at a school crossing when my youngest son came along the road towards me. He was wearing his new school uniform and showing off because his Dad was there on duty. I told him to wait at the kerb but he walked straight out into the road so I whacked him across his backside and dragged him back onto the pavement. Hell, that caused a stir because an elderly woman who witnessed the incident told me off, as did many other passers-by who reported the incident to my Guvnor. When I appeared in front of him I told him straight what had happened and that this was my child and that no one should interfere with my family or me. He agreed that it was my business and said that he would have taken the same action if it had been his son. And that was the end of that.

I drifted back into my hellish reality. I had now been in the same position for three hours. I was trying to keep sane. Tears of desperation trickled down my face as I lay on my back.

Suddenly I heard a car stop sharply, then the wail of a siren, and I judged that it must be close. They must have found my car with the door slung open as I had left it in such a hurry. The driver seemed to take ages to search the area; he was busy telling Information Room that he'd found the car. Then I saw a most welcome sight – a light flashed around the corner and with the light I heard the voice of my great friend Mick Jones. Catching sight of me in the beam of his torch, he put his hand on my head and said 'You're alright me old mate – your buddy is here now.'

Despite the freezing cold, Mick took off his overcoat, his tunic and his jumper, and wrapped me up like a Christmas parcel in an effort to keep me warm until the ambulance arrived. He later said he thought I wouldn't have lasted much longer as I was suffering from advanced hypothermia. He accompanied me to Edgware General Hospital, by now it was 4 o'clock in the morning, and once he knew I was in a stable condition, he got back into his car and sped round to my house to break the news to my wife, Margaret.

As soon as she saw Mick, she knew that the night she had dreaded all the time I had been in the police force had arrived.

Margaret hurriedly dressed and Mick drove her to the hospital, trying to comfort her by telling her I was in a stable condition. By the time they arrived, my clothes had been removed like armour, frozen solid. My body temperature was gradually brought up to normal and some x-rays were taken. Then, oh bliss, I was tucked into a lovely warm bed. But just as I was drifting off, a doctor arrived and I was pulled one way and pushed another.

The findings were not what I wanted to hear. The right kidney was split and bleeding (it took ages to be put right again), my backbone was shattered beyond repair, the spinal cord was intact, but a large piece of bone was stuck between the vertebrae causing paralysis. No one dared remove it.

While I was in hospital, my friend Mick never missed a single day without contacting me. When he could not visit, he spoke to me on the telephone. His friendship meant a lot to me and I could not thank him enough. Tragically, some years later, he died of stomach cancer, on my birthday.

Chapter Two

HOSPITAL WALLS

I lay in hospital for a long time wondering what would become of me. Although I could not move my head and arms, I felt nice and warm as if I was hibernating for the winter. The bruising had gone, I had no pain because I was paralysed, but I knew that I had a long way to go.

One bright morning, nearly a month after the assault, the surgeon came to see me and explained that he was going to stretch my spine to try to release the trapped bone. I was placed on a stretching contraption, straps were put on my chest and legs, and the machine sprung into life pulling the top half of my body north and the bottom half south. It was Christmas time and I remember feeling like a Christmas cracker.

After a few days of this treatment, I got the feeling back in my legs, the splintered bone was moved and I began to learn to walk again. The kidney on my right side was repaired so the 'big chief' said I could go to the police hospital in Hendon for final treatment and convalescence.

I had a steel corset made to help me to walk and, after proving to the doctors' satisfaction that I could walk properly, I was sent home, but with a proviso that I return each day for physiotherapy. I was also set a programme of exercises that I had to do on a daily basis. I followed it religiously because, in the back of my mind, I wanted to go mountaineering again.

For some time my wife and I had helped to run a mountaineering and camping club for boys and we did a lot of volunteer work for all sorts of underprivileged children, raising charity money for hundreds of youngsters from all walks of life.

Coming up over the following Spring bank holiday was a trip to the

Lake District and to my beloved mountain, Helvellyn.

So, after many weeks of recovery and physiotherapy, here I was again, back in the Lake District, and despite my bad back I pulled on my boots and gear and headed off up Helvellyn. It was a long haul up the mountain, but it was even harder work concealing from my family the agony I was feeling. I had had difficulty in even putting my climbing boots on, and they felt heavier and heavier as the day wore on. By the evening they felt as if they weighed three tons.

We sat and rested on Striding Edge, which stands about 3,000 feet up, on a narrow ledge about 18 inches wide, when all of a sudden some Airforce jets came screaming by. We were able to look down into the cockpits as they rounded the valley below, before they swooped out of sight. A wonderful moment: but my back was worse than I thought and consequently I had to be helped down from Striding Edge, which was difficult for my friends and me. I was in agony and was greatly relieved when I finally reached the bottom of Helvellyn.

I felt I had to overcome the pain and fear sparked off by my attack, and I had thought that by climbing that mountain I would achieve a lot. And I did. It proved to me that whatever happened in the future, I had climbed not only that mountain in reality but also the obstacles in my mind.

Back home again after my trip to the Lake District, I had an appointment with the surgeon. I did not dare tell him what I had been up to. But after my next visit, the following week, I suddenly collapsed, again paralysed from the waist down.

Climbing Helvellyn had caused more damage to my back than I had realised. I was taken from Edgware General Hospital to Stanmore Orthopaedic Hospital where this time I remained flat on my back for several months, during which time I underwent a series of x-rays involving liquid dye being inserted into the spine to show up any abnormalities. Sure enough the x-rays showed large breaks in two vertebrae. The surgeon, Mr Tricky, told me he was at a loss as to what to do next and that my circumstances were precarious. I lay there for several months and my treat in the summertime was when, still lying in my bed, I was wheeled round the hospital gardens.

Our house was miles away in Hendon and my wife had great difficulty visiting me at the hospital. She could not drive a car, so every day after finishing eight hours' work in the office in West London, she took the train to Edgware Road tube station, then boarded a bus to the hospital where she had a long walk through the vast grounds to my ward. After spending the evening with me she made the long journey home to prepare dinner and do all the daily jobs that are necessary when running a home.

My Chief Superintendent was informed of the difficulties she was having and arranged police transport for her, until he was replaced and the arrangement was stopped – something to do with costs, they said.

Nonetheless, Margaret continued to visit me every night without fail, but it put a great strain on her. She had an excellent job at British Airways with a salary to match, but the strain of being the wife of an injured policeman became too much to endure. She had reached breaking point and could not keep going at that pace – so she decided that she had no alternative but to hand in her notice.

Meanwhile, I did not seem to be getting any better. I had a great deal of time to think about not being able to walk again and I was often reduced to tears. I kept telling myself that I would fight this and win but, as I tried and failed, I became very downhearted.

One day after many months struggling and not succeeding, Mr Tricky, my consultant, told me about a well-known orthopaedic surgeon who specialised in back problems. He was based at Great Portland Street Orthopaedic Hospital in London and would be coming to see me.

When the day finally arrived for my appointment with Mr Kirwain, I was full of trepidation. Would he have to break it to me that I would never walk again? I almost did not want to see him.

He was a man of very few words and he said nothing as he studied my notes and x-rays before examining me. We then sat in silence for what seemed like an hour, but it was probably only a minute, before he gave his judgement. He said, 'Don't worry Mr Beard, I'll fix you up and you will be able to walk again.' I was beside myself with relief.

Within a few days I was transferred to Great Portland Street Hospital where I underwent another series of tests. A room full of orthopaedic consultants, registrars and house officers examined me and asked me many questions. I felt like a guinea pig for the day in their teaching class, but I wasn't bothered because it was the least I could do, after all they were doing for me. I knew that these skilled doctors were going to put me back together again. Mr Kirwain explained to me and everyone gathered in the room that the two breaks, of the type called 'dog neck breaks', were on the inside of my spine. Debris from the crushed bones and splinter-like fragments moving towards the spinal cord were causing the paralysis.

It was decided that the debris would have to be removed and a channel cut on both sides of the vertebrae to release the pressure on the nerves. Unfortunately, some of the nerve root ends were damaged beyond repair.

'Nil by mouth' stated the sign above my head on the morning the operation was due to take place. I had an injection in my backside to help me to relax and then I was wheeled into the anteroom next to the operating theatre. Another injection in my hand sent me into a peaceful slumber.

I woke up in the recovery room. It was in complete darkness – or so I thought – yet it was only 3 o'clock in the afternoon. I couldn't see properly because I had very high blood pressure so I was transferred to the intensive care unit, where my condition was monitored until my blood pressure returned to normal.

Back in my ward I found that a tube had been inserted in my back. I was lying on two rubber sheets – one fixed to the bed and the other left loose to help the nurses slide me from side to side on the bed. I had to lie for two hours on my left side, two hours on my back, and then two hours on my right side. I was moved like this day and night for 15 days and, Lord, it was excruciating. Those 15 days plus a week of therapy gave me time to recall my past, from the day I applied to join the police force.

Chapter Three

IN THE BEGINNING

I had first thought of becoming a police officer after my demob from the RAF in 1955 but never got round to applying and took a job in civvy street instead. By 1964 I had spent seven years of my working life as an engineer. I was thirty years old and in need of a change, so when I read an advertisement for recruitment to the Metropolitan Police I saw my chance and grabbed it before it was too late. My application to join was successful and on a cold and frosty morning in March 1965 I drove from my home in Nottinghamshire to the Recruiting Office in Borough High Street, London.

On the way there I thought back to my rebellious childhood and how I had ducked and dived to avoid going to school and getting an education. My father had left school when he was eleven years old; but that was when his real education began. He learned to play four musical instruments and taught himself to speak several languages. He was like a sponge, devouring any book he could get his hands on. He became a match for any scholar. One of my two sisters went to college after leaving school, but me… I kicked against authority and the discipline of school and refused to learn. I thought I knew better and I am sure that my school teachers were not too unhappy when my time came to leave.

Soon after leaving school I was conscripted into the Royal Air Force for two years' National Service. It was whilst I was in the RAF that I met two men, Air Marshal Sir Ivor Broom and Group Captain Burberry, both of whom had a great influence on my life. They warmed to my enthusiasm and the way I could undertake any task that was given to me with the minimum of instruction or fuss. They taught me how to look at things in a different light and encouraged me to get an education. So I followed their advice and during the course of my RAF service I knuckled down and passed the Civil Service Examination as well as a number of other educational examinations that stood me in good stead in the future. These two men were later to become very good friends of mine.

So here I was, driving from Nottinghamshire to London for my interview to join the Met. Police. I was going to 'The Big Smoke'. For someone who had lived most of his life in small Yorkshire and Nottinghamshire villages, driving through the London traffic was harrowing but I eventually crossed the Thames and made my way to Borough High Street.

After parking my car, I approached the Recruiting Office with great trepidation. Once inside, I was led by a uniformed police constable to a large hall where I was relieved to see other young men in civilian clothes. On the whole they looked uncomfortable, nervous and very green. The constable explained to us all in a booming voice that this was not a holiday and then proceeded to read out a schedule of times for lessons, examinations, medical tests, and drill. We were then dismissed and shown to our sleeping quarters, which were very basic but as I could sleep on a clothesline I knew they would not present a problem. I also knew that, after the disciplined and structured life of the RAF, I would have no problem with the routine laid down for us.

After unpacking our belongings we were summoned to dinner. This presented us with a good opportunity to get to know each other and a few of us sneaked out after the meal to see the bright lights of London town. We were drawn to Piccadilly where I was mesmerised by the crowds and the sights of the West End. We had one (or two) beers in one (or two) pubs and then found our way back to our bed, where we slept soundly.

The following day we rose early and were herded into a room where we were graded like turkeys. Some were weighed, whilst others were measured. We had our eyes tested and unfortunately some of my new colleagues fell by the wayside because of poor eyesight. There then followed the 'grab and cough' test, which I remembered so well from my RAF days! The Medical Officer instructed us to 'stand on those marks on the floor and bend over' and then proceeded to look up our backsides – to see if our hats were on straight, I think. We then had to stand upright and the MO tapped us on the chest one by one to make sure we hadn't contracted the dreaded tuberculosis that was rife at the time. Next we had to sit with one leg crossed over the other and in turn we were bashed with a bloody big hammer on the knee to test our reflexes. The final medical test was a foot check. In the 1960s you had to have healthy feet, they were your most important assets to propel you along the pavement. There were no panda cars in those days.

After the medical we went into a room where we had to sit a written examination. What I did not know at the time was that, having passed the Civil Service examination in the RAF, I did not need to sit this one! When the examination was over, we were ushered one at a time into a room where three high-ranking police officers wearing uniforms covered with silver braid were sitting with pens at the ready.

When my turn came, one of the officers said 'You seem a little old to become a police officer, Beard.' (Would you believe it, this from a man twice my age!) I bit my tongue and rather than tell him what I thought of his question I replied 'I believe that at thirty years of age I have had more experience than most of the youngsters here who have applied to become police officers. I am capable and willing to learn whatever is necessary to become a first class policeman. My training in the RAF will be an asset to the police force.'

A second officer asked me if my family was supportive of a move to London. My swift reply was that my wife would respect my judgement and that she and my lads would follow me to the ends of the earth.

When my results of the written examination were brought in, the three senior officers formed a scrum. They studied my answers in silence for what seemed like ages before the third officer said, 'I see you've passed, and with only one incorrect answer. By the way, *we* don't know where the source of the River Thames is either.' I felt sure that this lack of information would not hold me back when arresting hooligans in London! No more questions were put to me, and without further ado I was dismissed. I collected my expenses and drove 115 miles back to my family.

A few weeks later I received a letter advising me that I was in excellent health, that I would be accepted as a police constable, and that I was to report for training on 31st May 1965 at the Hendon Training School. So on 30th May 1965 I once again headed back to the great Metropolis to begin my new career.

I was very sad at the thought of my family being in Nottinghamshire whilst I was at the Training School. I knew it would be a great wrench, even for a short period, but I had to remind myself that I was doing it to make a better life for us all.

Chapter Four

BACK TO SCHOOL

I had hated my school days, and here I was, at the age of 30, back in the classroom.

Our intake of recruits had been split into two Classes, one to be trained at Peel House in Regency Street, the other at Hendon Police College in North London. I was in the latter group, which suited me because Hendon is at the end of the M1 and was much closer for me to get to Nottingham to be with my family at weekends.

Before being despatched to our respective training centres, we were taken to Scotland Yard where we were shown into the office of Assistant Commissioner Andrew Way, whose massive frame, as he sat behind his desk, seemed to fill the room. He looked directly at me, then his gaze swept over the rest of the recruits before coming back to me. I could imagine him thinking, 'An old man with a load of kids still wet behind the ears.'

He drew himself up to his full height and you sensed immediately that he was a man who did not suffer fools gladly. In a voice full of authority, he said *'The primary objects of an efficient police officer are the preservation of life and the protection of property'* and he then proceeded to explain in some detail what this meant. When he had finished, we all took the oath of allegiance to Her Majesty the Queen by swearing on the bible to uphold the laws of the land. We took the oath with much feeling; we had come a long way to get this far and it meant a great deal to us.

After taking the oath we were dismissed and our Class was taken to Hendon College where we were issued with bedding, uniforms and a police number. Mine was TS 798 (TS standing for Training School).

Hendon was to be our home for the next six months.

The officer in charge of Training was Chief Superintendent Tom Wall who gave us a short introductory lecture. He had apparently been a good copper in his time and was known throughout the Force for his acerbic wit.

Then we were taken to the classroom where for the next few weeks I did my cramming: learning, learning, and more learning under an excellent tutor, Inspector Thornton, before passing the examination at junior level.

At my age I found studying difficult but I was determined to succeed because there was a great deal riding on my getting through the training. My family had sacrificed a lot for me, I was missing them, and reading the daily letters from my wife Margaret and the boys made things even harder. Nonetheless, I kept going because I was doing it for them.

I soon got into the routine of getting out of bed between four and five o'clock in the morning to do some cramming before going to breakfast. As the weeks passed I was thrilled to learn that all the hard work was paying off and I passed the intermediate examination without much difficulty.

Towards the end of our training, Sergeant Shipley took us to a training centre in Hertfordshire. There we saw a house built of real brick with real furniture inside. The doors and windows were wide open. Pointing to me, Sergeant Shipley shouted, 'You are my volunteer.' He then ran round the outside of the house throwing smoke bombs in through all the openings. Then he came back, grabbed me and told me to go inside the house and rescue the occupants. By now, smoke was belching from every orifice of the building and it looked as if it really was on fire.

Throwing caution to the wind, I ran towards the house and as I got as near as the smoke allowed, I got down on all fours and crawled through the front door. The smoke was so thick I could not see a thing in front of me and I felt my chest tightening as it filled my lungs. Suddenly, there was an enormous, crash, flash, and bang – the loudest I had ever heard – and my eardrums felt as if they had been blasted out of my head. Unbeknown to me, Sergeant Shipley had thrown some firecrackers into the house to add realism to the situation. I ran out of the house holding my head and with my eyes streaming.

When I reached the others who had been watching, Sergeant Shipley shouted at me, 'Serves you bloody well right – you didn't turn off the gas or electricity or check for any danger to yourself. You are a dead copper and dead coppers can't save lives!'

Of course he was right, and I felt very sheepish. It was a lesson well learned. I felt sure that if ever I became faced with a similar situation in the future I would remember that it was all very well being courageous but it was more important to assess the situation before making any decisions that cost me my life or other peoples' lives. In fact, I dealt with many fires during my service so I was very grateful to Sergeant Shipley.

Then it was back to the classroom again, learning about the various Acts and sections of the law, which we were required to be able to quote 'parrot-fashion'. The knowledge I gained this way was to stand me in good stead on many occasions throughout my service.

One situation that stands out in my mind was when a villain put a meat axe into another man's head, causing him to lose an eye. After a good deal of investigation, I arrested the culprit and he was charged with assault. He was dealt with at the Old Bailey and during the hearing I was asked if I knew the definition of assault. Confidently, I quoted the law which states: *'An assault is the intentional application of force by a person on another, without his consent, or the threat of such force, whether by act or gesture, if the person threatening has, or causes the person being threatened to believe that he has, present ability to effect his purpose.'* The Judge stopped me there and told me that he was impressed with my excellent memory.

We were given tests almost daily and as we were rapidly approaching the end of the thirteen-week course we were learning and re-learning, cramming into our brains as much information as possible in preparation for the final examination. On the day of the examination, we were herded into a room where we were informed that 120 marks were the highest that we could achieve. So, pens out and heads down, we were off and writing until the Instructor shouted, 'Pens down, stop writing'. After a short break, which seemed to pass very quickly, it was back into the room for the second half.

We had to wait until the following afternoon for the Instructor to announce the results of our efforts. I thought my marks would be about 100. He called out our names, with the results in reverse order, and to my despair 100 went by, then 111, 112, 113, 114 and 115, still without calling my name. I began to wonder if he had missed it or maybe even lost my papers! He then added that he was pleased to announce that PC 798 (me!)

had scored 119 points out of 120 – and asked me what happened to the other mark! I may have been the oldest recruit in the class, but boy was I the proudest, and the thought came into my head, 'Thank you Air Marshal Sir Ivor Broom and Group Captain Burberry for making me learn and get an education to offset those wasted days at school.'

That evening we all went out for a good 'booze-up' and visited quite a few pubs in the Victoria area. Afterwards we made our way back for a very good night's sleep.

The following day, as arranged, my wife Margaret and our two sons travelled down to London to meet me and we spent a wonderful day in town before driving back to Nottinghamshire, weary but very happy. I took some well-earned leave and we had a great few days just spending time together.

All too soon, my leave ended and I headed back to London. Along with one or two other recruits, I was posted to 'A' Division and told to report to the Divisional Commander at Cannon Row Police Station. He assigned me to duty at Gerald Road Police Station in Belgravia and I was allocated sleeping quarters in Vernon Lodge Section House, Hyde Park, which was to be my home for the next few weeks until I found accommodation of my own.

Chapter Five

GERALD ROAD POLICE STATION

On arrival at the Station, we were wheeled into Superintendent Newman's office. 'How far do you think you'll get in this job?' he rasped. 'I'll be happy with your job', I replied. I could tell he did not appreciate the joke.

I served under him for a long time but our relationship was not a good one. I had no respect for him at all and I am sure the feeling was mutual. He went on to receive a knighthood and became the Chief Constable of the Royal Ulster Constabulary before being appointed Commissioner of the Metropolitan Police, but I was never impressed with him.

I remember the time when our two families lived near each other. His wife and mine became friends and they used to go to the Women's Institute together. He called me into his office one day and told me to tell my wife to keep away from his because police constables' wives do not mix with officers' wives. I lost my temper (which did not do me any favours) and told him 'If that's what you want, you bloody well tell her yourself!'

After my meeting with Superintendent Newman, I reported to Sergeant Plumbley who was to be my Section Sergeant. He was a real gent, a great man, who had a row of medal ribbons on his chest, awarded to him for service as a desert rat during World War II. He was one of the nicest men I've ever known and he couldn't do enough for his colleagues. Nothing was too much trouble for him and he was always happy to help people. This was his role in life. I was deeply saddened to learn of his death some years later.

'Plum' took me on a tour of the Station and introduced me to some of the other sergeants, namely 'Marc' Marcantonio, who had an answer for everything, 'Wally' Wotherspoon, an expert on vice, and 'Sailor' Bowers whose nickname spoke volumes. I was also introduced to a few older constables, some of whom were affectionately as 'Station loafers'.

The following day was to be my first day of learning beats. I was allocated the number PC A394 and I was paired with a senior constable and we had a school crossing patrol to look after at noon. Whilst we were engaged on seeing children across the road we were informed that a robbery had taken place at a jeweller's shop in Bond Street and that not only had the two robbers stolen a great deal of jewellery but they had also hijacked a police car. They had crashed the car in South Eaton Place (not far from where we were on duty) and decamped.

We were advised that they were heading our way, so we ran up the road to try to cut them off. As we did so, we saw them in a garden on our right hitting a police constable with Indian Clubs. Unfortunately, the garden was protected by eight-foot tall iron fencing with big spikes on the tops of the railings.

The PC I was with ran all the way round the fence to get into the garden but I decided that he would take too long to reach the attackers so I decided to climb over the railings. I managed to get to the top but unfortunately I lost my grip and slipped. One spike went right through the palm of my hand and another pieced my uniform and entered my stomach. I pulled my hand off the spike, lifted myself off the other, and then climbed down into the garden to assist in the arrest of the two villains.

Back at the Station, Sergeant Plumbley was preparing charges against them for theft and assaulting a police officer when he noticed a trail of blood on the Charge Room floor and followed it into the room where I was standing and saw that it ended at my feet. Opening the top of my trousers I found to my astonishment that blood was oozing from a wound in my stomach. My hand was also bleeding. 'First day out and badly injured!' An ambulance was immediately sent for and I was taken to St George's Hospital at Hyde Park Corner where a very pretty nurse stitched up my wounds. I couldn't help laughing when she pushed a bottle brush through the hole in my hand to clean it out.

As a result of my injuries I was signed off sick for two weeks. I thought, this can't be bad, one day's work and two weeks off! But the time soon passed and back to the fray I went. This time I remained uninjured long enough to get to know the area better.

On one occasion I was out learning beats with PC 'Dinger' Bell when he asked 'How do you expect to catch criminals with those great hobnailed boots on? Villains will hear you coming from miles away.' I took his advice and had my boots re-soled and heeled with rubber.

A few nights later, now walking quietly round my beat, I made my first arrest. She was lying in the gutter, extremely drunk. I had paid good money to have rubber soles and heels put on my boots but she was so drunk that I could have passed by driving a steam roller and she wouldn't have heard a thing. It transpired that the lady in question was Sir Winston Churchill's daughter.

On night duty I was partnered with PC Wally Hammond, who to this day is still lurking around Belgravia Police Station after nearly half a century of police work. At about 3.30am, we went into Victoria Coach Station and sneaked onto an empty bus to have a quick ciggy. Before we knew it, we both dropped off to sleep. We must have slept for some hours because the next we knew was when we woke up with a start and saw that the bus was going across Putney Bridge – several miles off our beat!

We quickly moved down the bus and Wally tapped the driver on the shoulder, giving him a terrible fright. Once we had peeled the driver off the ceiling of the bus he managed to stop the vehicle but he was still shaking when we got off and I am sure that to this day he is still wondering how we came to be on his bus. Unfortunately for him, we had no time to offer an explanation. We should have reported off duty at Gerald Road Police Station by 6am but it was now 6.30 so we grabbed the first taxi that came by and made our way to the nick. 'Chasing a suspect, Sarge,' we shouted as Sergeant Plumbley watched us getting out of the cab. The trouble was, we had forgotten that he had been a police constable himself and no doubt he had a very good idea what we had been up to.

I spent many good days on the beat with my old friend Wally but my period of learning beats with other PCs soon came to an end and it was time for me to go it alone.

My first posting on my own was to No.4 Beat covering a large area of Belgravia, including Hyde Park Corner. I was walking along feeling as proud as Punch when a member of the public stopped me. 'Where's St George's Hospital, mate?' I knew it was on my beat but for the life of me I couldn't remember where it was. I ought to have done because I had been a patient there and had been sewn up by a nice little nurse who also stuck a needle in my bottom! As I was consulting my 'Guide to London's Streets' that I had bought for occasions such as these I heard someone say to my enquirer 'Where do you want to go to, mate?' Would you believe it, the hospital was at Hyde Park Corner, only about 100 yards along the road. Boy did I feel an idiot.

My disorientation was probably due to the fact that I had been taken out of a small Nottinghamshire village (Cropwell Bishop) and suddenly dropped into the centre of London. I got lost on several occasions during the following months.

Most of my off duty time was taken up with studying. I still had a long way to go and I was expected to pass one examination a month in preparation for a final examination at the end of my two-years' probation. Even though I was working very hard both on and off duty, I had some marvellous moments on the beat and I should like to tell you about some of them.

One night, my beat took me past Brompton Church and the vicarage. As I approached the vicarage just before dawn I noticed that some of the ivy above the vicarage wall had been disturbed. The ivy was directly over a box where the dustbins were kept. I looked at the situation for a few moments then, as my eyes grew accustomed to the darkness, I saw a picture lying on the ground. I walked over to it and saw it was a painting of Sir Robert Peel, the man who had been responsible for the formation of the Metropolitan Police in 1839. I laughed out loud and thought, 'They can't fool me like this, I'm too long in the tooth to be caught.' So I walked around the corner, waited a couple of minutes and then strolled back. By the time I got back, the picture was gone and I thought about my colleagues back at the nick and told myself, 'If they think I'm going to fall for this, they've got another think coming.'

I then headed back to Gerald Road where, to my surprise, no one said a word about the picture. So neither did I. At the end of my shift I just went home to bed.

The following evening as I strolled into the Station, a few minutes ahead of the time to parade for duty, I heard someone yell '394, my office, *NOW!*' I wondered what I had done wrong. I followed my Sergeant into his office where he told me that a burglary had taken place the previous night on my beat – at the vicarage – and that some very valuable pictures, including one of Sir Robert Peel, had been stolen! 'Oh no,' I thought, 'what have I done?' The Sergeant continued, 'Just be more vigilant in future – check your beat.' 'Yes, Sarge,' I replied quietly.

Later that night I was walking along Semley Place where there was an ancient block of flats with underground coal cellars. As I passed, I shone my torch into the cellars and my eyes focused on an unusual shape – a very large shape. On closer inspection I saw that it was a body, no, in fact, it was two bodies, both naked, and they were in a very compromising position. A naked man was lying on top of a naked lady! I crept closer and saw that they were two local tramps who were performing a sex act. But what concerned me more was that they had built a fire in the cellars; it looked very dangerous and appeared to be out of control. I became extremely concerned for the safety of the inhabitants of the flats above the cellars and immediately called for the Fire Brigade. As soon as they arrived I took the fire chief to one side and led him to the scene and shone my torch on the two tramps who were still 'performing'. Without any hesitation he unreeled the water hose he was carrying and, pointing it directly at the two lovers, fired a jet of water at them, scoring a direct hit. As the water hit the target, the man jumped so much that his false teeth shot out of his mouth across the cellar floor and hit the far wall. Neither the fire chief nor I could contain our laughter.

The two lovers dressed as quickly as they could. Meanwhile, the brigade doused the flames and after making sure the cellars were safe we all went our separate ways.

One night, I was told to keep an eye on a large house in Eccleston Square. It was in the process of being renovated and contained a goodly amount of materials, timber, bricks and the like, but some of it had apparently gone missing. I noticed that the basement door was open so I went in and searched the building for intruders. The house appeared to be uninhabited so after carrying out a fruitless search I found a newspaper, laid it over some bags of cement, sat down, and lit a cigarette. I was enjoying a quiet smoke, without a care in the world, when all of a sudden the bags moved! There was a loud moan and as I jumped up in shock, I thought, 'Bloody hell, the cement is alive!'

I dropped my ciggy and shone my torch around the room. Well, I got the fright of my life as someone emerged from beneath the newspaper. It was one of the local winos! Without realising it, I had been sitting on him – and very comfortable he was, too.

After I had pulled myself together, he begged me to let him stay where he was in the warm. I agreed, on one condition – that he told me who was stealing the materials from the house. Thus it was that in the early hours of that morning I recruited my first *snout*, and the information he gave me later on led to two arrests.

⬤ ○ ⬤

Soon after I arrived at Gerald Road Police Station, someone told me that, as part of my training, I would have to attend St George's Hospital and find out where the mortuary was located, to meet the mortuary attendant, and to observe the basic procedures for dealing with corpses. Unbeknown to me, someone from the Station telephoned the mortuary attendant and told him that I was coming to see him for 'training'.

When I arrived at the hospital with a colleague, we went to the mortuary attendant's office for a brief chat and a cup of tea before making our way downstairs to the mortuary. Opening the door, the attendant said, 'Now this is where we keep the bodies,' and walking across the room to a set of drawers set in the wall, he took hold of the handle of one of them, gave it a tug, and it slowly slid open. Now, I expected the drawer to contain a corpse but I wasn't ready for what happened next because it suddenly sat up and said 'Aaaah!' as a breath of air came out of its lungs. I can tell you that I ran out of that room as if my life depended on it. When I stopped to catch my breath I could hear shrieks of laughter coming from the mortuary and it slowly dawned on me that someone had played a big trick on me. Excellent, I thought, and stored it away in my mind to play on some other green constable in the future.

My colleague and the mortuary attendant then explained what they had done. Rigor mortis had already set in on the body the attendant had chosen for the 'trick'. He had pumped air into its lungs and fastened a spring to its back so that when the drawer was opened the body sprang into the upright position, releasing the air in its lungs at the same time. It was the 'Aaaaah' that had terrified me. As the mortuary attendant left the mortuary, I quickly followed and when I reached the door I locked it behind me, leaving my colleague prankster on the inside. He screamed to be let out, which I did after a few minutes, at the same time telling him never to play a trick on someone if he couldn't take a joke himself.

I took every opportunity to tell a joke or to play a trick on my colleagues. With such a potentially stressful job as ours, I believed it was important to have a good laugh and I think that is why I was able to enjoy my police service so much. By looking at situations in a different light, it is always possible to see the funny side of things, rather than taking them too seriously. I was known as a prankster and the Station jester but became even more so after I played the following trick on one colleague.

Kieren Murphy, a young Irish lad who had recently qualified as a police constable, asked me a question. He had come to me for advice because in his eyes, I was as an 'old hand'. He was not aware I had been in the service only one week longer than he had! Anyway, this young lad had fallen in love with a woman police constable based at Gerald Road Police Station and he desperately wanted to marry her. He had only known her for about three weeks! I thought to myself, he should give it more time because he could be buying a pig in a poke. However, I told him to type a report containing all the facts about wishing to marry his WPC and to end the report with 'I respectfully ask for your permission to take her hand in marriage.' I advised him that the report should be addressed to Superintendent Newman, the Station Commander.

Away Kieren went and typed out the report, declaring his love for the WPC and ending it as I had recommended, with copies for the Commissioner of the Metropolitan Police and the Divisional Surgeon (as I had also recommended!). He then made his way up to Newman's office, and in the meantime I made the quickest exit I have ever made and hid but not for long. 'BEARD – MY OFFICE, NOW!' shouted Newman. He was absolutely furious at the trick I had played on Kieran. I innocently told him that I had merely followed the procedure laid down in the RAF, in which it was necessary to obtain your Commanding Officer's permission before you could get married. 'GET OUT OF MY OFFICE,' he screamed. As I left, I chuckled to myself as I imagined him pondering on whether I was as naïve as I made out, or just plain stupid.

About this time, my wife and sons had moved down to London and we were all happy to be a family once again. We had been allocated a flat in Gower Street, off Tottenham Court Road, but unfortunately, to put it mildly, it was not very nice. Soon after we moved in we ordered a television set which was duly delivered, but because the flat was in the basement the set would not work so it had to be returned to the shop. A day or two later there was a knock on the door. I opened it to find an official-looking gentleman standing on the doorstep. He told me that he was a Post Office TV Licensing Officer and that he had come to check that we had a current TV licence. I told him that I didn't have a licence as I didn't have a TV. He did not believe me and told me that I was committing an offence. He left, announcing that he would be back again to see my licence.

True to his word, two weeks later he returned and asked if he could come in. I refused, whereupon he thrust a summons in my sticky paw (I had been painting) and kept on asking me if he could come in until I finally agreed. He then asked where the television set was, to which I replied that we didn't have one and that we hadn't had one since coming to London. He immediately changed his tune and asked me to give him back the summons. I could see that he was getting hot and bothered so I continued to refuse and told him that I was prepared to go to court to see what the Magistrate thought of the situation. Eventually, feeling sorry for the man, my wife intervened and made me give the summons back to him. However, that was not the end of the matter.

We later moved to a better flat in Belgravia and I ordered a television set. When it was delivered, the engineer programmed it in. Down to the Post Office I went, to purchase a licence, taking with me the licence reminder that was four months out of date. I showed it to one of the clerks who told me that the licence had to be backdated to the date of the reminder. I let him fill it out and then told him where to stuff it. He chased me out of the office and along Ebury Bridge Road demanding his money, but to no avail. I then went to Ecclestone Street Post Office and again asked for a TV licence. A current licence was issued and paid for. Now, at last, I was able to sit down and watch television in peace and comfort.

We were happy in our new flat. My sons went to St Peter's Primary School and later attended Archbishop Tennyson School in Lambeth. Meanwhile, my wife got a job at BOAC and by the time it had become British Airways she had been promoted to a very good job which enabled us to travel to a number of countries, including the USA, Africa, the Caribbean, and Australia where I visited my mother. My party piece when asked what my wife did at British Airways, was to reply: 'She kick starts all the jet engines.'

Sometimes I was sent to Hyde Park Section to patrol the interesting areas of that great open space. On one such occasion I was walking near Rotten Row when I saw two people on a park bench engaged in an activity not permitted under the Park Regulations.

They were performing a sex act – in broad daylight! I approached them and told them to get up and leave the park immediately. You can imagine my amazement when I saw that they were in fact two women. They ran off as soon as I confronted them but I made them come back to collect the garments they had left behind on the bench. Although it was the promiscuous Sixties, to a somewhat naïve man from Nottinghamshire this was something new. I hadn't realised that this sort of thing went on in London's Royal Parks but I can tell you that I have since gained much experience and my horizons have certainly been broadened since those early days on the beat.

On my next posting to the Park, I was paired with another officer. The sun was at its hottest that day and when we reached the Serpentine we stood watching the bathing beauties for a while (just to make sure that they didn't get into difficulties, you understand). We strolled round to the attendant's office where we knew we could get a nice mug of tea and rest our weary feet for a while. Because it was such a hot day, the attendant asked us if we would like to borrow some swimming trunks and towels and go for a swim. We didn't need asking twice and as quick as a flash we had changed into the gear plunged into the cool water.

After a refreshing swim, we hopped onto the bank to dry ourselves and to catch a bit of sun. Suddenly, out of the corner of my eye, I saw the Duty Officer from Gerald Road. Before we could take any action, he spotted us and said, 'What do you two think you are doing?' 'Observation, Sir,' I replied. 'What observation?' I thought quickly and said, 'Well, the attendant told us that there have been a number of thefts here, so he suggested that we put on some swimming gear and blend in with the crowd.' Luckily, the Inspector fell for it hook, line and sinker, and in a different tone of voice said, 'Do this for another thirty minutes and then report back to me with your findings.' He then walked off. My partner took one look at me and said, 'What a bull-shitter you are Beard, but thank goodness you are a quick thinker.'

I told him to look over to his left and discreetly observe two lads who were definitely 'at it' – theft that is. We recognised them as local 'tea-leaves'. We approached them and told them that they were nicked. They took one look at us and one said, 'Pull the other one.'

My partner showed them his warrant card and they started to run away but before they could make good their escape we grabbed hold of them and searched their belongings. Sure enough, they had purses, wallets and jewellery in their rucksacks. We locked them in the attendant's cubicle, quickly got dressed, and went back to the nick. The Duty Officer was there and we told him what we had done.

'Good work lads,' he said, 'Charge them.'

Chief Superintendent Gilbert was also at the Station and I overheard the Duty Officer explain how the arrests had been made. He told him that in view of the high number of thefts in the swimming area in Hyde Park, he had instructed us to change into swimming gear and mingle with the crowds and that within an hour his plan had worked and two thieves had been arrested. The Chief Superintendent complimented him for using his initiative – and it wasn't long before the Duty Officer was promoted!

I was on patrol one night with PC John Hodson. We were walking around his beat checking doors, shops, unoccupied premises, etc., when we arrived at Young's, the world-renowned fishmongers, in Elizabeth Street. Now, as all coppers know, locked doors don't give, but there inevitably comes a time, when you least expect it, that a door will give way and you go flying inside. John took hold of the door handle of Young's premises, and promptly fell into the shop. 'Someone's in here,' he said, 'let's search the place.' Gingerly, we went inside and looked around. We didn't need our torches because we could see quite well.

We went upstairs and entered a room. Something moved and we saw man standing at the window. Without a word, John drew his truncheon, threw it at him and, *Bang!* he went down, out like a light. I switched the light on but there was no one to be seen. We searched the room – no one there! We looked in the cupboards, under the table, and even in the drawers – still no one. It was a complete mystery. How could the man have got past us? We just couldn't work it out.

All of a sudden, John let out a howl because lying on the floor, flat as a pancake, was a cardboard cut-out of a fishmonger. Our mystery intruder had been a display model but it was now minus its head because John had knocked it off when he threw his truncheon at it. The truncheon was nowhere to be seen, it must have gone clean through the window and landed in the coach station below. After we had secured the premises and left I asked John, 'Do you always get your man like that?'

The Fox public house in Passmore Street, Pimlico, was on my beat. I knew the landlord's daughter Diane because my wife usually spent an evening in The Fox once a week. One day, Inspector Jan Caels called me into the nick and what he told me caused me to hot foot it down to the pub. I entered, in full uniform. The pub was full of customers and Diane was being rushed off her feet. She took one look at me and shouted, 'Get out – do you want me to lose all my customers?' I said to her, 'If you talk to me like that you *will* lose all your customers and I will close you down.' She began to argue and became abusive so I took her to one side and told her to calm down and listen. 'I've just been informed by my Inspector that you do not have a licence to serve intoxicating liquor,' I said. 'Oh yes I have, I'll show you,' Diane replied, and off she went to get the licence. She rushed back and, thrusting it in my hand, said 'There!' I replied, 'So it is, and it expired last Wednesday, just as the Inspector has said.' She went a little pale. I told her, 'We are not closing you down but the Guvnor will give you until tomorrow evening to renew your licence.' She quickly rang her solicitor.

I'd been directing traffic for a couple of hours in Kings Road, Eaton Square, Belgravia, and was feeling ready for a break, when I saw my Relieving Officer strolling towards me. I stopped the east and westbound traffic and turned to start the northbound traffic. (I must point out that there is no southbound traffic at this junction because it is a one-way street with four lanes of traffic going north.) Nothing moved when I waved them on, so I waved a second time. Still nothing moved. I looked towards the east and saw a car speeding towards me. I stepped into its path and signalled the driver to stop. Nothing happened, so I stepped out further into the road but the car swerved around me, hit the kerb, and came to rest on the pavement. 'What the hell do you think you are doing?' I shouted at the driver. I was shaking because he had nearly hit me. Then I saw a woman in the car. It was obvious that she was about to give birth and was clearly at the point of no return. I moved quickly and got her into a more comfortable position, while my colleague called for an ambulance. One soon arrived and the crew delivered the baby in the car. Mother and baby were then transferred to the ambulance and taken off to hospital, the husband following in his car. Two near misses in one go. Throughout my eventful career, I never did get to deliver a baby.

One night at 10pm, a Police Constable was posted outside an off-licence in Wilton Road, Victoria, because earlier that evening it had been broken into and bottles of booze had been stolen. Allegedly, two lads had smashed the plate glass window by throwing a piece of concrete at it, stepped inside, taken the drink, and run off. During the course of the night, the officer on guard had to be relieved for a meal break, so another officer was taken to the scene in the police van and assigned to guard the shop. Whilst he was on watch, a lady in the house next door offered him a cup of tea and he drank it while standing in her doorway. The lady was very attractive and he was so taken with her that he forgot what he should have been doing and failed to notice the time passing.

When he eventually dragged himself away (with the promise of a date at the Rialto the following Thursday) he was astonished to find that the shop window was completely devoid of booze! He radioed through to the Sergeant who informed the Duty Inspector who was responsible for making out a report of the incident. The following day, an Investigating Officer was appointed to find out what had happened and his findings were as follows:

The first PC was put on a report for being absent from his place of duty.

The second PC was put on a report for leaving his post and for not being on the beat he had been assigned to.

The van driver was put on a report for failing to book out the van. He was also put on a report for failing to book it back in.

The Section Sergeant was put on a report for failing to supervise his men.

The Station Officer was put on a report for failing to ensure that the records of the Transport Book were properly kept.

The Duty Officer was put on a report for failing to supervise his men.
The Sergeant was put on a report for failing to report the crime in the Crime Book.
The PC on communications duty was put on a report for failing to record the messages from the scene; and as this officer represents the Station Officer, he was put on report again.

The outcome of the affair was that:
The two thieves were happy to supervise the theft of the booze.
The Officer in charge of the Station kicked the backside of the Duty Officer, who in turn kicked the backside of the Station Officer, who in turn kicked the backside of the Section Sergeant, who later kicked the backside of the van driver.
The van driver was reprimanded.
The two PCs were each fined two weeks' pay.
This is called 'Line management.'

<hr />

By this time, I was coming up to my six months on the beat and so I was expected to spend a few more days back at school, followed by an examination to see what I had learned about the job.

Chapter Six

STILL A LOT TO LEARN

Now we go back to Gerald Road Police Station and a lovely Sunday morning – well it was lovely until this next incident!

A woman whose husband had left her with three children all under the age of four was at her wits end and in a traumatic state. She took the three toddlers and put them on the parapet of Putney Bridge, and as they moved they eventually toppled over the edge and fell into the Thames.

I was walking towards Chelsea Bridge at the time. Sergeant Gross arrived in a van with several officers who were placed at strategic positions on the bridge to watch the river as it flowed past. As we kept watch, a police boat arrived and sat in mid-stream. I looked down and saw what appeared to be a rag doll floating face up on the water towards the bridge. I knew that if I acted quickly a life could be saved – if only I could get near enough to help. In a flash, and without thinking of the consequences, I ran across the Bridge and jumped over the rail into the Thames, shouting to the other PCs as I went over. I hit the cold water and started to sink. God, what had I done!

The police boat moved towards me. I was stuck in the mud up to my waist unable to move, but luckily for me the tide was going out and I could just keep my head above the water. The body of a little girl floated past me and it was picked up by the boat crew who worked tirelessly to revive her, but in vain. She was dead.

The police boat could not get close to me because the water was too shallow and it would have run aground. The water level was now down to my chest and I could only watch and wait to be rescued. I tried again and again to pull my legs out of the mud but to no avail. When the tide had receded, ropes were thrown to me. I tied myself up and the heaving began until I was eventually pulled clear of the mud and hauled up a 20ft wall. In spite of my terror, I laughed when they pulled me up because I came out of the mud like a cork out of a bottle.

Once more on dry land, I stood there stinking like a cesspit, or worse. When I asked for a lift back to the Station, back came the reply, 'Not bloody likely!' and suddenly the area was devoid of policemen. I staggered back to the nick on my own and as I made my way there people kept stopping and looking at me, but when they caught a whiff of me they quickly moved out of my way.

Back at the Station, I was hosed down and once again vaguely resembled a police officer. My Sergeant suggested that it might be a good idea to make my way home (on foot, would you believe) to get washed and changed.

Well you can imagine what my wife said when I rang the doorbell upon arrival home. The gist of it was 'You're not coming in here dressed like that!' She made me take off my smelly, wet clothes outside the front door and passed me a black plastic bag to put them in. Then, and only then, was I allowed in. I felt like a naughty little boy and slunk into the house. When she ran me a nice hot bath I knew I had been forgiven!

Afterwards, I sat and thought about the traumatic day I had had. I didn't care or think about the stupid thing I did, jumping in the Thames. I had done it, instinctively, for the small child. I also thought how desperate the mother must have been to do what she did. By law, at that time, she was immune from prosecution for one year and a day after giving birth and therefore she was not held responsible for her actions.

It made me think of my own children – on that day three young lives had gone forever.

'And God will wipe all tears from their eyes and death shall be no more.'

I was becoming aware of people who suffered from harmless delusions. We had our share of them on our patch.

A Polish refugee named Stanislav stopped me one day and pushed me into a building, saying in broken English, 'Come, come, I show you Nazi murderer.' I followed him into an office block and then into a room where he turned and said 'He's gone.' Then the door swung open and the Manager came in. 'That's him,' shouted Stanislav. The girls in the office were laughing and someone said, 'That's another one caught.' The Manager told me that Stanislav came in most days and accused him of being the Camp Commandant of Stalag 99 somewhere in Poland. I put my arm round Stanislav's shoulder and gently led him outside. After a chat he went merrily on his way, not knowing what he had done. The young typists who were laughing in the office were not old enough to be aware of the tyranny, looting and murder that had been carried out by the Nazis during World War II. I found out later that Stan's family had all been wiped out during their terrible ordeal in concentration camps; only he had survived, and he was left mentally unstable.

Another such case was when I was patrolling Knightsbridge near the Post Office in Wilton Street. An old lady said to me in broken English, 'Come quick, a large fire, people trapped.' Then she ran off. I followed. She ran along the street, turned left, then ran along another street until we were back where we had started. I leaned against the Post Office wall, took off my helmet and mopped my brow. I asked her how she knew there was a fire and she replied, 'I heard the bells.' I asked her where she heard the bells and she replied, 'In my head.' Recalling the incident with Stan, I thought 'Bloody hell, another one', and it emerged that she, of course, was another poor soul who had suffered at the hands of the Gestapo and had experienced the atrocities of War. We had a long chat and it was clear that she hadn't realised what she had done. I walked her to her home and we parted company.

I had a good friend, Koln, a German Jew, whose father had sent him to college in England in 1939. Both his parents had been doctors in the 1930s and they had many German patients. When the War broke out, all the members of Koln's family were arrested by what he called 'the Bosche'. The children were killed because they were of no use to the Germans, and Koln's parents were murdered when they had outgrown their usefulness. Many traumas arose out of such cases as these, resulting in great unhappiness, hospital treatment and either mental breakdown – or death, as in the following case.

A colleague was called into some woods and found a man hanging from a tree. He had tied a rope around a branch, then tied it around his neck, and jumped. God, he nearly pulled his head off! Investigation on behalf of the Coroner revealed that he was Jewish. During World War II he had been held in a concentration camp, separated from his family, but he had managed to survive only because of his skill as a cobbler. After the War, he had travelled all over Europe looking for his family. Sadly, he had discovered that most of his family had been killed, but he was led to believe that his brother and sister were still alive. His search came to an end when he finally learned that they had suffered the same fate as the other members of his family. He then took his own life.

$$\sim\!\!\!\Rightarrow \text{\large O} \Leftarrow\!\!\!\sim$$

Getting back to my beat, it was certainly a gorgeous day for a stroll round London town. I was happily window-shopping, not realising that I was way off my beat, when who should come into view but the Duty Inspector. (He had been following me, I learnt later.) I thought to myself 'How do I get out of this situation without being bawled out.' Then I saw a villain I knew, sitting astride a large Honda motorbike. I knew for certain that he had no driving licence so I grabbed him and said, 'Eric, you know that you've got no licence.' He had no choice but to admit it, which was lucky for me because the Inspector had just joined us. The Inspector knew I was off my beat and said 'You were window shopping Beard, don't try to deny it,' to which I replied in my best 'butter wouldn't melt in my mouth' voice that I had been in pursuit of a suspect, having spotted him on my patch, and that I had been looking in the window because I could see his reflection in the glass. The Inspector thought for a moment, then looked into the window where he could see the whole street reflected in the glass and said 'Good work, Beard, carry on.'

Eric was found guilty of driving without a licence and, to top it all, the bike he had been riding had been stolen a few days earlier, so he had been well and truly caught red-handed. The Inspector reported the incident to the Commander and I was later told to report to the Commander's Office. When I arrived, both officers congratulated me on my initiative and said the arrest was the result of was an excellent piece of detective work. I was later awarded a Commander's Commendation. Good job they were not aware of the truth or I would have been getting a reprimand instead of a commendation!

On another occasion I was on duty with PC Ralph Griffin, a new recruit, showing him the job – the blind leading the blind, some might say. Ralph was an ex-Army paratrooper and a keen officer. On the previous day I had taken part in the annual Metropolitan Police Barking to Southend Race-Walk Championship, a distance of just over 33 miles. My feet were sore, to say the least, and the tops of my legs had almost seized up, so my objective was to find somewhere comfortable and quiet in which to pass the time. I knew just the place – we would walk by the residence of Lord Hall of Tonypandy in Eaton Mews because he always invited PCs in for a drink, so off we headed in the general direction of the Mews.

As we were approaching his Lordship's house I spoke to Mrs Graham Hill, his next-door neighbour, who was with her baby on her doorstep, the baby being the future Champion racing driver, young Damon. Lord Hall saw us and immediately invited us in and poured us each a whisky. He certainly had the gift of the gab and before we knew it, we had been with him for over three hours – it was time to go.

No sooner had we left than an old lady called to us. She told us that she had a terrible crime to report – she had seen someone on a No.38 bus get off without paying the fare! I knew this lady of old, she was very lonely and would find any excuse to have some company. She asked us to come into her very smart residence in Eaton Square, so in we went and she poured out two large glasses of whisky – it was always whisky in Belgravia.

When I looked at my watch again, it was 10.15pm. We gulped our whisky straight down and no sooner had we left the house than we bumped straight into a man loitering around outside and looking into some of the basements. We approached him and when he spoke it was clear to me from his accent that he was from my native Nottinghamshire. I asked him what he was doing in this neck of the woods and he explained that he was just taking an evening stroll. During the course of being questioned he admitted that he was claiming unemployment benefit and I half jokingly said, 'I bet you've had the DHSS over in Nottingham.' Well, to my astonishment, he answered, 'Yes, how did you know?' He added that he was successfully claiming benefit in Nottingham, Derby and Grantham!

We promptly arrested him and returned to the nick to face a furious Sergeant. (A Section Sergeant cannot go off duty until all the men on his shift have been accounted for.) We apologised for being late but explained that it was because we had made an arrest. He calmed down and told us to charge the criminal.

Before he went home, the Sergeant asked if I had been drinking, to which I replied that it was only for medicinal purposes as my body was not quite what it should be after the charity walk. I wasn't able to pull the wool over his eyes. He said, 'You must think I was born yesterday; just get the charge completed and then go home.' *Phew, got away with that one, but you'll get caught next time, Beard,* I told myself.

I rang Nottingham CID who dispatched an officer to collect our prisoner. Meanwhile, I put him in a cell and went off duty. Ralph, the rookie cop, asked me how I knew that the criminal had fiddled the DHSS. I told him it was just a gut feeling and I had been right to trust my instincts on this occasion.

The following day, I was on the beat in Ebury Bridge Road when an Irishman asked me where the monastery was. As I didn't know of any monastery I directed him to the nearby Roman Catholic Cathedral in Victoria Street. I felt sure that one of the clergymen there would be able to tell him where the monastery was. Then the Irishman's friend chimed in saying 'No, we want the Monastery, the Monastery of Labour.' God help me, we were standing outside the Ministry of Labour! They both went in, thank the Lord.

I stood there for a couple of minutes having a quiet chuckle to myself, when a dopey (and I mean dopey) housing estate porter called out to me. I knew him well. He was one of those people for whom everything goes wrong. He shouted 'Jim!' I thought to myself, 'What now?' I turned and saw he was killing himself laughing. You can always tell if a person is an idiot because they tend to laugh to themselves about absolutely nothing. Anyway, he said to me, 'An old lady on the estate called me into her house and gave me a bomb. She told me it had come through her roof during the war. It hadn't gone off at the time and so her husband had put it on the mantelpiece as a souvenir. It had been there ever since but it started to leak a white substance from a crack in the case. Her husband had died and she asked me to get rid of it.' He went on, 'I put it in my pocket to take it to the nick. On my way I stopped off at the bookie's to place a bet. I showed the bomb to them and would you believe it, they all disappeared. I left the bookie's and made my way to the nick and, guess what, they did the same thing there. The Sergeant jumped over the front desk and ran.'

I said to him, 'A good job you got rid of it, then.' He said, 'No I didn't, Jim, I've still got it here.' With that, he put his hand in his jacket pocket and what should he pull out but a 10lb bomb! Well, at that point I needed clean underwear. We were in a street full of people, the shops were full of shoppers, the roads were full of cars and bikes and, to top it all, two Irishmen had just been looking for the 'Monastery of Labour!' What should I do now with a loony caretaker and a bloody bomb due to go off any minute? Please tell me, Lord.

He answered my prayer straightaway. Someone at the Police Station must have decided to take action after all, because from out of the blue, two cars and a van with lights flashing and horns blazing, screeched to a halt at my side. One man jumped out, grabbed the bomb, jumped back into his vehicle and dashed off towards Chelsea Bridge. I waited for a bang and gradually relaxed. I must admit I could have done with one of Lord Hall's large whiskys.

I told the idiot at my side that if he ever pulled a stunt like that again I would throw him in the end cell, lock him up and throw away the key. He still couldn't see what he had done wrong or understand that he had put lives in danger. I later told his wife, who was a Government secretary, and she remarked 'He has been a lunatic all his life; when I go out of an evening I have to put him to bed.' Oh, how the other half live!

The Police Service is often expected to act like all of the emergency services rolled into one – I'll explain.

I was on duty when a woman called me into her home. She had received a wooden box from Ireland and she was suspicious of it because she did not know anyone who lived in Ireland and she thought that perhaps the box might contain a bomb. As I entered her front room, she thrust the box into my arms, more or less pushed me out of the front door, and then banged the door shut behind me. I carried the box very carefully to a large open space, which was deserted. I kicked the lid off the box and dived out of the way very speedily. Well, I can obviously tell you now that there was no bomb in the box, but to my surprise and relief, it did contain a large fresh salmon. I closed the lid and went back to the lady who had *kindly* handed me the box. I knocked on the front door and when she answered her face fell when she saw I still had the box. I immediately told her that there was no bomb but there *was* a salmon. She snatched the box from me and pushed the door shut in my face without saying a word of thanks. My thoughts went something along the lines of 'the ignorant bitch, not even a thank you.'

To top it all, when I went back to the nick for refreshments, I opened my lunch box only to find that my wife had given me fish paste bloody sarnies to eat!

I was called to a posh house in Belgravia. A lady came to the door and said, 'Can you get this thing out of my house.' I went in looking for the 'thing'. I wondered whether it was a cat, a dog, possibly a monkey, or even a crocodile, but there, before my eyes, lying on the floor, was a lady looking very dishevelled. Her eyes were closed and she looked as drunk as a Lord. This stinking lady was a tramp and was well known around Victoria Station. The owner of the house shouted at me in a very loud voice, 'I want her out, I want her out. It's your job to get her out.' I replied, 'Oh, is it? What's she doing here in the first place?'

The grand lady explained that she had asked the employment office to send someone to do some washing up and they had sent this woman. She had ordered her to clear up the kitchen, which was stacked high with dirty dishes. Some time later she had gone back into the kitchen to check the woman's progress, only to discover that she had apparently found a bottle of vodka in the store cupboard. She was just downing the last drop when the householder entered. The householder ordered the woman to leave immediately. She got up off the chair, walked very unsteadily towards the door, but did not make it that far and, as if in slow motion, she leaned against the wall, slithered slowly down it, and fell fast asleep on the floor. The householder then said to me, 'You must get her out, I'm expecting some very important guests shortly and it just would not do to have this, this *thing* here when they arrive. Get her out now!'

By this time the Grand Dame was really getting on my nerves. Nonetheless, I telephoned my Sergeant at the Station and asked him what I should do. He replied that it was not really our job – unless I felt I wanted to help. I most certainly did not want to help. I repeated what my

Sergeant had said and she blew her top – 'I'm going to telephone my husband, he's a magistrate you know and you have to do what he says.' When her husband arrived, having been summoned by his wife, he asked her what was going on. She explained in very dramatic terms. When he asked me for my side of the story I told him what had happened and added, 'I wouldn't let this woman past my front gate, let alone into my house. It's your job to eject her from your premises, not a matter for the police.' He was obviously not satisfied with what I told him and telephoned my Inspector. I was made to wait outside the front door.

When the Inspector arrived I told him the full story. The Inspector then went inside, spoke to the couple and reiterated what I had told them about ejecting the woman. We then left. I have to add that if they had treated us properly we would have been happy to help them. Oh, and by the way, they didn't get rid of the old biddy for another two days!

I was coming to the end of my first year as a probationer and, boy, had I crammed a lot into that year. I loved every minute of being a constable in the Metropolitan Police and I counted my blessings for being in such a rewarding job. But the time had come for my First Year exam, so back I went to Training School for a week.

Chapter Seven

GETTING TO BE AN OLD HAND

I had successfully passed my examination and was back on the beat. Ambling round Chester Square, I saw a lovely old lady standing in the doorway of her house. We exchanged a bit of banter and she asked me if I'd like a cup of tea. How could I refuse? It gave me an opportunity to rest my 'plates of meat' and have a nice hot cuppa. The lady was very charming and obviously quite lonely. She rang for her maid who in no time at all returned with a pot of tea and some delicious bacon butties, which I devoured with relish.

After a lovely chat with my new-found friend, I looked at my watch and realised I would have to leave because my Sergeant would be checking up on me. The lady went with me to the door and I thanked her for her hospitality, but I apologised for not knowing her name. She smiled and replied, 'Mrs Chamberlain.' It was not until I was walking away that I realised she was none other than the widow of Neville Chamberlain, the pre-war Prime Minister who, you will recall, returned to Britain in 1939 after visiting Adolf Hitler at his home in the mountains in Germany. He got off the aeroplane, waved a piece of paper in the air and proclaimed, 'Peace in our time!' (He should have worked at Gerald Road Police Station!)

So now I could boast that I had breakfasted with Mrs Neville Chamberlain and that she and I, a lowly police constable, had that very morning discussed what was going on in the world and that between us we had put it all to rights.

It was a fairly nice day. Two of us were strolling round the beat and as we came to Ebury Street we heard a very loud explosion. I could see from the smoke that the site of the blast was a small bed and breakfast hotel. We ran to the scene as quickly as we could. When we arrived I saw a naked young man lying on the pavement. He had been blown out of the second floor window. He was dead.

I then saw a young girl, also naked, who had been blown out of the same window, but she was still alive. She had fallen on to a large ornamental spiked iron fence at the front of the building. One of the spikes had pierced the inside of her thigh and was protruding from one side of her buttock. I got as close to her as I could and wrapped my coat around her because she was shaking, either from the cold or shock, I could not tell which. I held her body weight as best I could and tried to comfort her. There wasn't much bleeding but she was obviously in great pain. It was not long before she became unconscious with her head resting on my shoulder. I held her as if she was my own child and I wanted to take the pain away from her. Her face was very beautiful, unmarked by the terrible explosion.

A very long time seemed to pass (it was probably no more than 15-20 minutes but it seemed longer) before an ambulance arrived. I was getting very tired and the girl was becoming heavier and heavier, but I dare not let her move or her injuries would have worsened. Even when the ambulance crew arrived, they had to wait for the Fire Brigade to follow with cutting equipment. Meanwhile, there was not much they could do apart from giving her an injection to reduce some of the pain. A table was built round her with cushions and blankets until she was completely surrounded with supports. The cutting began by using a grinder; the noise was deafening, and frightening.

The girl had to be supported for an hour before she could be lowered from the iron fence, still with part of the railing in her body. I thought at the time that it was fortunate that she was unconscious, otherwise she would have never have been able to withstand the pain. She was placed in the ambulance and I felt great relief, but also a great sadness knowing that her life was lying in the balance. My coat was returned to me and the ambulance drove away with its siren blaring. The young girl eventually had the spike removed from her body and when she was fully recovered her parents took her home.

The hotel was still burning an hour or two after the two young people had been removed from the scene. We learned later that there had been a gas explosion. The gas supply was cut off, the Fire Brigade extinguished the fire, and what was left of the building was made safe.

It was quite some time later that an inquest into the death of the boy revealed the circumstances. He and the young girl had been engaged in love-making when their gas cooker exploded and the force of the blast blew them both out of the window.

A chance in a million, which left one young lover dead and the other lucky to be alive.

⎯⎯◗ ◖ ⎯⎯

Still in my second year of probation, and life was never dull. On a beautiful autumn day, I was patrolling with PC Mick Smith in Hyde Park. Mick was a Welshman from the Rhondda Valley. We were happily walking along Rotten Row, deep in conversation, when all of a sudden we saw a young girl half sitting in the centre of the Row, on the sand. She was obviously drunk and, would you believe it, she was filling her knickers with sand. We recognised her as one of the local prostitutes. And I nearly collapsed with laughter when Mick said, 'That'll be a bit rough on her customers, boyo.'

Mick and I lifted her up and walked her to the Police Station, but as there were no women police officers at Hyde Park Station she had to be taken on to Paddington Police Station where there was a Matron. I accompanied her to the Charge Room and sat her down on the bench seat until Matron arrived.

After a body search, I took her to the cell. Just as I was leaving the cell, she jumped up and screamed. I turned round to see what the problem was and, boy, I wished I hadn't because she threw the heaviest punch that I'd received for many a year. Her left hook connected with my mouth and I must admit I saw stars for a moment. I instinctively pushed her away because I could see another left hook coming. She was still very unsteady, owing to the amount of drink she had consumed, and she lost her footing and fell on the seat. As she did so, she hit her head against the wall and I rushed to her aid to see if she was all right. She burst into tears (if there is one thing I can't stand it is the sight of a woman crying, it really gets to me) and in a drunken voice murmured, 'I'm so sorry, I didn't mean to punch you.'

At that moment, the Duty Officer came to see what all the commotion was about. Well, the woman and I looked a right pair – me with a fat lip and blood dripping onto the cell floor, and she with a lump a big as an egg on the back of her head. I had some explaining to do but luckily the Duty Officer accepted my explanation.

Whenever I saw my 'sandy' friend from Rotten Row whilst on the beat, we always stopped for a chat and we had mutual admiration for each other. Boy, could she pack a punch!

A few weeks later I was on Early Turn when a call was received in the Communications Room from BOAC requesting urgent police assistance. I was ordered to attend and on arrival I was confronted by a couple of stewardesses and a very frightened young Arab boy. Evidently the boy had just arrived in the UK on a flight from Cairo. One of the stewardesses told me that the boy had been put on an aeroplane in Egypt the previous night and he had found his way from Heathrow Airport, by bus, to the Victoria Air Terminal. Lord knows how, because he couldn't speak a word of English.

As I approached him he took one look at my uniform and fled in terror into a corner of the room. I persevered but since I couldn't speak Arabic I drew a sequence of pictures showing an aeroplane departing from one airport and arriving at another. Eventually he relaxed and began to trust me.

So now I had a twelve-year old boy on my hands and we made our way to the Police Station carrying his two tatty suitcases. He clung to me like grim death, especially when he saw all the policemen and women in uniform. I took him to the canteen and gave him some food; he was ravenous. Then we made our way to one of the offices and I telephoned the Egyptian Embassy. I got through to one of the staff and described the situation to her. She asked to speak to the boy on the telephone but when I tried to hand the telephone to him he again ran into a corner, shaking like a leaf. I walked over to him with the receiver held in my hand and as I got closer to him he heard the sound of Arabic coming out of the earpiece and overcame his fright. He listened carefully and smiled when he recognised his native tongue. He grabbed hold of the phone and looked all over it, wondering where the lady was – he could hear her voice but was totally baffled.

I placed the telephone by his ear with the mouthpiece at his mouth and when he understood how this strange contraption worked, he happily chatted to the Embassy official for some time. We had to stifle our laughter at what he did next. He took the receiver over to his tatty suitcases and 'showed' it what they were like, walking round them a couple of times to make sure that the telephone had 'seen' them. He then passed the telephone back to me. I tried to compose myself as the official at the Embassy told me that the boy had lived all his life in the desert and that he had never seen a car, a ship, a telephone, or an aeroplane until the day previously. Living a nomadic sort of life, the only people he had come into contact with were his family and that was why he had been so frightened of all the white people at the airport.

Apparently, he had been sent to England to be educated. The Embassy staff had been expecting him for two days and they had become quite concerned when he hadn't arrived. I took him to the Embassy and he gave me a big hug as I was leaving; I could see tears in his eyes and he was clutching in his grubby hands the pictures I had drawn for him when we first met.

I dined out on this story for years afterwards. It still brings a smile to my face all these years later. I felt a certain fondness for the 'little prince'. God only knows what would have happened to him if he had gone out into the big city by himself. That day I was definitely in the right place at the right time (I think my Sergeant would have added, '...for once.')

The Force did not have personal radios in those days so we had to look out for the light flashing on Tardis-like police telephone boxes. On one such occasion I answered a call from a box connected to Chelsea Police

Station and the operator asked me to go to Ennismore Gardens to see the occupier of No.22 who wished to report an incident. On my way to the Mews I saw a lady coming towards me holding two leads in her hands. My eyes went to the ends of the leads and I saw two bloody great, ferocious-looking lions. I wanted to run away but you can't do that when you are wearing the Queen's uniform. The lions started to follow and it was not long before they had closed in on me. I thought: as soon as I say anything, those sods will eat me, but in a very feeble voice I said to the lion lady, 'Get those lions out of here to a place of safety, NOW!' She told me that they were her little pets and that the little darlings would not hurt me. I again ordered her to get them off the streets. Thankfully she immediately took them home.

Some time later the lady was killed in an accident in the Brompton Road, together with one of her beasts. After her death, the other pet was put down.

My next call was to a house not many streets away from the scene of the lion incident. I knocked on the door and a woman answered. She said, 'I've got two pet snakes which I keep in the airing cupboard.' I thought, 'Fine, but please get on with the story, I'm ready for my lunch.'

'The problem is, they are not there any more,' she added. Well I cannot stand snakes so without further ado I informed her that, unfortunately, it was not really a matter for the police and advised her that I would contact the RSPCA on her behalf. I went out of that house like greased lightning.

I found out that the person who assigned this job to me knew my phobia about snakes and he had purposely not told me on the telephone what the call was about. I think he knew that I would have refused to go to the house. That afternoon we received a call from the lady to say that the RSPCA had recaptured the snakes – they were found up the chimney!

These two incidents remind me of the story of the police constable who saw a man walking along the road with a gorilla. The officer stopped the man and told him to get the gorilla off the streets, as it was a danger to the public, and take it to the zoo. The man promised he would do so.

The following day, the officer again saw the man walking with the gorilla in the same road. He stopped him and said 'I thought I told you to take the gorilla to the zoo, yesterday.' The man looked puzzled and replied, 'But I did as you said, Officer, I took him to the zoo yesterday, and today he fancies a trip to the cinema to see *Jungle Book*.' (Such is life.)

➤ ◑ ◀

I was called into the office one day and informed that I was to undergo a firearms course. I had carried a gun on duty on many occasions whilst guarding Government Ministers, Embassy officials, and the like. The only instruction I had received up to now was 'You put the bullets in there and they come out here' so it was probably about time that I had some proper training. Some bright spark had obviously decided to send me on a course before I shot myself.

Off I went to Old Street Police Station to be assessed. I had been a marksman in the RAF so I knew the basics but I had to learn the police system. The Instructor gave each man six rounds of ammunition to fire and he assessed each of us in turn in the different techniques of using firearms.

When he thought we were competent, we were taken to another range where a film was projected onto a screen. The rules governing the firing of a weapon are that if a gunman threatens life, you shoot him; if he threatens innocent bystanders, or if innocent persons shield him, you take cover. So when it was my turn, a gunman appeared on the screen and, *Bang!* I fired. The Instructor shouted, 'No, no, no. Come here you bloody idiot, look at the screen.' I looked again and saw the gunman was holding a baby as a shield. 'Now let's look where your bullet went.' Would you believe it, the bullet had gone straight into the gunman's forehead! The instructor remarked, 'Well, that *was* a lucky shot.'

We then went to another range, at the end of which was a house with four windows and a door facing the front. On the way leading down to the house were places to hide behind. Twelve ropes were attached to twelve cardboard targets. According to which rope was pulled, a target appeared depicting a scene such as a gunman standing at a window or behind a door, a gunman with a hostage, a vicar, a child at a window or a door, and so on.

Just as the Instructor was explaining this to us, Sir Joseph Simpson, the Commissioner of the Metropolitan Police, arrived to see for himself how the new training was progressing. Two Instructors were detailed to give him a demonstration. The Inspector in charge had to pull one of the ropes and the other Instructor stood on the range ready with his loaded weapon. The scene was set to impress the Big Chief.

When the signal was given, the Inspector pulled a rope and the first target to appear was of a gunman holding a hostage. The Instructor on the range ran for cover, but he did not quite make it. As he ran down the range he tripped over his own size 10s, hit the floor and, *Bang!* his gun went off. The bullet went deep into the roof of the range. After a few seconds, the Commissioner turned and said, 'Very nice, good job you were using blanks.' No one dared to enlighten him.

On the second day of the course we were taken to a secret underground bunker somewhere in Essex. The bunker was designed for use by the Government in the event of a nuclear attack. There were stairs leading down to a room well below ground and it was dark and dank.

We were divided into two groups and issued with a weapon and blank ammunition. The first half went into the bunker and hid while the other half was instructed to go in and get them out, or shoot them, or bring out prisoners. When my turn came to enter the bunker, I went gingerly down the first steps, waited until my eyes became accustomed to the light, and then started to go down the second flight of stairs. I took only one step when there was a bright red flash of light and a bloody great *Bang!* Boy, was I sore and burnt. Some bloody idiot had stuck his revolver through the stair rails into my face and pulled the trigger. I had no eyelashes, and there were powder burns all over my face. (Well, it couldn't have made my face any worse than it was.) The exercise was eventually called off, but not before I had been bombed and shot at.

Back at Gerald Road again it was nearing Christmas. We enjoyed this time of the year and even though the weather was cold, patrolling was great fun. We received many invitations to parties and the drinks flowed everywhere we went. So many bottles of booze were given to us, or were delivered to the nick, that we just didn't know what to do with them all!

I remember delivering some bottles to St George's Hospital with PC Gerry Adley. The doctors and nurses who were off duty invited us into the doctors' mess. As soon as they had a few drinks they seemed to change from the sensible people we rely on so much when we are ill. Gerry was grabbed by three of the doctors and two nurses and held down while they encased him in Plaster of Paris from the waist down so that he couldn't move and he was completely in their power. He was taken on a tour of the wards and when they got to the orthopaedic ward, who should be there but our Superintendent. He immediately recognised Gerry and yelled 'Adley!' The doctors and nurses disappeared very quickly and Gerry was left trying to get up but he fell backwards and ended up flat on his back. Gerry shouted back, 'Merry Christmas, Sir.' Everyone burst out laughing, including the Superintendent, and Gerry's bacon was saved on that occasion.

Those naughty doctors and nurses found another victim later that day. A Traffic Patrol officer who had entered the hospital for some Christmas cheer was immediately set upon and covered in plaster. However, the nurses were not satisfied with just parading him around the hospital and took him outside. The story goes that they dumped him in Victoria Railway Station and left him there. I don't know to this day whether he was ever rescued, but I understand that he was never seen at St George's Hospital again.

One Christmas Day we went to the hospital in force: there is safety in numbers! We went round the wards with the doctors and nurses singing Christmas carols and it certainly made for a good Christmas, especially when we saw the faces of the little children light up as they listened to this motley crew of people in white coats and uniforms. This was a duty we loved doing best of all.

On a similarly festive evening, I was on protection duty guarding the Bolivian Ambassador at his residence in Eaton Square, armed with my trusty revolver and twelve rounds of ammunition. It was Christmas Eve and the Ambassador came up to me and said, 'There are two turkeys in the kitchen, cooked, go down and make yourself a sandwich.' I did not need telling twice and off I went to the kitchen and cut a huge chunk off the bird and made a delicious sarnie, which I washed down with some Bolivian wine the butler had provided.

At the time I was working twelve-hour day shifts – 6am to 6pm – and my friend PC Bob Brown was doing twelve-hour nights. There was a comfortable settee in the hallway so when Bob arrived to relieve me I advised him to relax for the night and told him about the Ambassador's invitation to help ourselves to the turkey. I then went off duty.

I dutifully returned at 6 o'clock the following morning to relieve Bob and he went off to bed. I was sitting reading an Agatha Christie thriller when, at about 8am, I heard someone screaming. I immediately got to my feet, drew my revolver, and began running in the direction of the screaming. It was coming from the kitchen and as I approached with infinite care I came face to face with ....the cook. She was hysterical and, pointing at the kitchen, she screamed, 'We have had a robbery!'

I went into the kitchen and checked all the doors and windows. To my relief they had not been tampered with and there was no evidence of a break-in. I turned to the cook and asked her what all the fuss was about. I soon learned what all the fuss was about when I turned and saw two naked turkey rib cages on the kitchen table, looking very forlorn, with all the flesh picked cleanly off. You've guessed it, my colleague, Bob, had taken up the Ambassador's invitation and had a snack. Well, not exactly a snack, he had eaten both turkeys. They had been intended to grace the Ambassador's table for Christmas dinner. Would the fact that all of the Ambassador's cold turkey had been eaten by the British security services lead to a cold war with Bolivia, I asked myself? I really did not know what to do next and rang my Sergeant at the Station for some well-needed advice.

As I waited for him to ring back I crossed my fingers that he would come up with a good suggestion. Well, he did. He rang round the local Police Stations as well as a nearby prison and, thank goodness, one of the prison warders at the prison offered to help us out. After what seemed like hours, but was really only about 30 minutes, there came a knock on the back door and there stood a prison warder with a beautiful cooked turkey in his hands. Without further ado, the turkey was put on the table in place of the two bald specimens and we beat a hasty retreat out of the kitchen.

Judging by the 50 bottles of Scotch and the 25,000 cigarettes the Ambassador later delivered to the nick, I don't think he ever found out about our little scam. Bob Brown was not allowed anywhere near the booze or cigarettes after the stress he had put his colleagues through that day.

I went on duty one afternoon but the Sergeant sent me back home with instructions to change out of uniform into plain clothes and go to Victoria Station with five other officers for observation duty. We occupied various strategic positions around the Station where we stayed for about seven hours. Around 10pm we emerged for a toilet break and for refreshments. We were ravenous.

As we sat down on a bench munching our food and talking, two men entered the railway station and began acting suspiciously. They were going from person to person, trying to mug them. I said to my colleagues, 'Stay there, keep watch, I'm going to see what they're up to.' I got as close as I could and saw the two men pounce on an innocent man, pin him against the wall, and demand money from him. I could clearly hear what was being said and it was obvious to me what they were doing. I knew there was enough evidence for arrest.

The two 'muggers' were talking with Irish accents. I signalled to my colleagues and went up to the two and asked what they were doing. In the space of a couple of seconds, I was belted in the stomach and as I doubled up in agony the same guy brought a beautiful upper-cut to my face, splitting my gums, lips and nose. Blood spurted out as I sank to the ground. I was soon on my feet again and as the man who had hit me went back to the business of mugging, I grabbed hold of him, put my arm around his neck and frog-marched him straight into the nearest wall, letting go just before he hit the wall. He ended up, down and out, with blood to match mine. The second man saw what was happening and moved in, but by then my colleagues had joined in the fray and the two muggers were arrested and taken to the Police Station where they were charged with four counts of robbery.

When they were searched, one of them was found to have £360 in his belt. We found out that he was a professional boxer and that he had recently won a bout at The Sporting Club of Great Britain and had a great future in boxing. Unfortunately, he had expensive tastes and was impatient for the money to roll in from boxing matches, so he had resorted to robbery.

Both criminals appeared at Bow Street Magistrates Court the following morning, where the Magistrate asked after my welfare. I could not speak due to the injuries I had sustained when arresting the two criminals, so another officer spoke on my behalf and told him what had happened, using the notes I had made in my notebook. The Magistrate complimented me on my bravery and said he hoped I would soon be back to normal. The two villains got bail and they went back to Ireland, but before long they were caught again and this time they were each sentenced to two years' imprisonment. In the meantime, I was commended by the Judge and also received a Commissioner's Commendation for my actions.

Chapter Eight

VILLAINS BEWARE

Late one night, a message came from Scotland Yard for police to go to a three-storey private flat in Lowndes Square where a robbery was in progress. Apparently, five men had burst into the flat and tied the occupants up while they carried out the robbery. Well, they thought they had tied everyone up. In fact the family's young son was in his bedroom doing his homework when he heard the commotion downstairs. He dialled '999' and was clearly frightened, so the operator kept him talking. The boy was able to give a running commentary of what was happening. His father, mother, sister and housekeeper were lying on the floor, bound and gagged.

When we arrived, the crew of Alpha One, driven by PC Reg Butcher, was already at the scene. The building was surrounded and in we went, some entered via the rear fire escape and others through the main entrance. Police dogs were also brought in and one dog was taken to the rear of the property while the other was taken to the front.

Suddenly, someone came flying down the fire escape and landed at an officer's feet. He was promptly arrested and thrown into the van. Two more criminals emerged from the front entrance and they too were put in the van. A fourth member of the gang was arrested inside the flat. When we entered the flat, we untied all the occupants, the boy handed over the telephone and the Yard was informed of the outcome. The boy was commended for his coolness and for his bravery in contacting the police.

Meanwhile, one of the dogs was still in the flat and it kept on growling. It led its handler into the bedroom, growled, and then came out again. The handler asked the boy if there was a teddy bear in the bedroom

– the dog had a thing about teddybears – and the young lad confirmed that there was. No one thought about it any more until the dog went back into the bedroom and growled once more. Then all hell broke loose. The fifth member of the gang had been hiding under the bed and the dog had grabbed him. The man screamed loud enough to wake the dead because his arm was in a bad way, but none of us cared too much because the dog had done its job well.

The gang was sentenced to long terms of imprisonment in one of Her Majesty's 'hotels'. By the way, all five had been allowed into the UK following the Hungarian uprising of 1956!

During the week that this robbery took place I was posted one night on Station Gaoler duties under my old friend Sergeant Plumbley. It was a miserable night, the rain was pouring down so I was glad to be working inside. My first task was to check on the prisoners to ensure that they were all right.

In one cell, sleeping it off after having been arrested for being drunk and disorderly, was my old friend Stanislav. Stanislav, you will recall, was the man who had suffered at the hands of the Gestapo in Poland during the Second World War. He woke up as I entered the cell so I had a brief chat with him and brought him a cup of tea.

During the course of the night, more prisoners were brought in and when Sergeant Plumbley brought in another one I had to tell him that all the cells were full. He said, 'Let's see who we can release.' and picked poor old Stanislav who had been in for about seven hours. Stanislav was not a happy man when he heard the 'good news' that he was to be released and he made a right old fuss, kicking and screaming all the time. He was hopping mad and shouting, 'Where do you expect me to go this time of night, I can't get a bed anywhere, all the hostels are closed.'

Nonetheless, he was bailed to appear at Court the following day and he was still cursing and swearing at the Sergeant and begging to be allowed to stay the night as I saw him to the door. 'What do I have to do to stay?' he asked. Without thinking, I jokingly replied 'Throw a brick through the window!' It doesn't take a genius to imagine was happened next. Well, how was I to know that he would be daft enough to do something like that!

Sergeant Plumbley was sitting at his desk when all of a sudden there was a loud crash and the sound of breaking glass, and a nice new house brick landed squarely on his desk, smack bang on top of his mug of tea.

He was not amused. He dashed out into the street, grabbed Stanislav, and brought him back into the nick. He yelled at me, 'Beard come here now. You told him to do that, didn't you?' 'No Sarge. Would I do a thing like that?' I replied, Luckily, Stanislav did not let me down and did not confirm that the suggestion had come from me.

As a penance, I had to prepare a report on the damage for the information of the Surveyor's Department at the Yard. Stanislav, meanwhile, was charged with causing criminal damage and his reward was to spend a few more nights in the warmth of a police cell.

——◦◦——

The following night, we had a newly promoted Inspector in charge of our Relief. His name was Durston. As we stood on parade discussing the events of the previous twenty-four hours, in he walked. We didn't move so he bawled us out for not jumping to attention. Someone muttered, 'Who the hell does he think he is?' The Inspector's face turned red with rage and he shouted, 'If it's drill practice you want, then drill practice you shall have.'

For the next thirty minutes he marched us up and down the Parade Room shouting, 'Stand at ease. Attention,' about sixteen times. Someone muttered under his breath, 'He'll pay for this.' He must have heard it but did not say anything. Sergeant Marcantonio said, 'With due respect, Sir, you won't get much out of these lands if you carry on like that.' The Inspector flew off the handle and subjected us to another twenty minutes of drill, despite our mutterings.

He kept up this lunatic type of behaviour for a couple of nights and we kept out of his way as much as we could, not even coming into the Station for refreshments. As a result, very little work was done and he ended up searching the whole area for us every night, but he couldn't find us. One night he and Sergeant Marcantonio toured the area in the car and Marc told us afterwards that the Inspector was in a fit of temper when he couldn't find us. The Inspector ordered every officer to report to him in the canteen at a set time of night for his meal break so that he could be checked in.

On about the fifth night I was returning to the nick when I saw someone run out of Gerald Road carrying a bottle which he passed to another officer in Elizabeth Street. He in turn passed it to an officer in Chester Square. This happened several times and I wondered what the hell was going on but I thought it best not to ask too many questions.

Durston didn't report for duty the next night, or the next, nor on any other night for the remainder of this tour of duty. Rumour had it that his petrol tank had been filled with water, one bottle at a time. It certainly did the trick because from that day on he called a truce with the Sergeant and his men. He settled down and eventually became a good Guvnor. He worked well with us, helping us when we got into a mess, as a good officer should.

One clear night I was on my beat in Kensington when I saw smoke pouring from the roof of a large house. I thought it was a little odd as there was no chimney on the roof. I shouted to a passer-by to call the Fire Brigade and then entered the building, which was divided into flats, and immediately cleared the ground floor. I then smashed open another door and as I did so I remembered my old Training Sergeant telling me 'Dead coppers can't save lives.' I silently thanked him for those few words of wisdom. Entering the flat, I told the tenant to get out quickly. We both ran out into the street and when he had recovered his breath he told me that an elderly lady lived in the flat above his. I had no choice but to go back in, as the Fire Brigade had not yet arrived, and entered the building for a second time. I immediately found the gas tap and turned it off. My next objective was to get to the top floor and as I did so I thought, 'You bloody idiot, gas lingers', so I ran back down the stairs as fast as I could.

Suddenly, there was a massive explosion and the whole building shook, masonry and timbers flew everywhere, and windows shattered. The fire quickly took hold and the flames were roaring out of control. There was a second explosion shortly after so I kept well clear and warned the Fire Brigade on their arrival. I was very pleased to see them. They rapidly extinguished the fire and damped the building down.

The gas cooker was found to be the cause of the fire. The old lady had been doing some cooking and had suffered a fatal heart attack and twelve hours had elapsed between her collapse and the first explosion. I said to myself later, 'Thanks Sarge, you saved my life that night.'

Near misses such as these stay in your mind forever. I recall another occasion when I attended a fire, accompanied by PC George Frazer, a Scotsman, who was a good friend and an excellent copper. We broke into the house through the ground floor window and immediately turned off the gas and electricity, something I'll never forget to do. Facing us as we entered was a most gruesome sight. Part of a woman's body was lying across an electric fire which was fully lit. Her clothes as well as her back and legs were burnt. The rest of her body had been completely burnt away.

I opened the kitchen door and immediately smelled gas, so I went round to the back of the house, kicked open the kitchen door and let the draught blow the gas out of the house. Another life was probably saved that day.

We collected evidence for the Coroner, the body was removed, and we wrote up our notes. Investigation showed that the woman had dropped dead onto the heater, so thankfully she felt no pain from the burns.

One of the advantages of being a police officer was that the sporting facilities were second to none. We kept fit by swimming, playing football and cricket, and weight-lifting. I enjoyed playing bowls with Sergeant Marcantonio and Inspector John Dorking. We three regularly played for the Station team. I also did the annual 33-mile walk from Barking to Southend, accompanied by Gerry Adley and Mick Burnbrook. Mick always completed the walk, but unfortunately I didn't because I often got blisters. Yet I always enjoyed these walks as they kept us fit and at the same time we raised money for charity. I loved sport, my favourite being cross-country running. We did a 27-mile run and I was thrilled to win two competitions, one in South Wales and the other in Lincolnshire.

Chasing criminals required fitness. I could outrun many of them, even in my middle age, but I maintain you can run faster in the opposite direction if you are facing the end of a barrel of a gun, especially when it is pointing at you.

Fitness also makes for an alert mind and, my goodness, you certainly needed one at times. I remember the time my neighbour's two-year old daughter Amy walked out into the street to watch some workmen repairing the road. The steamroller fascinated Amy so much that she became hypnotised by it and started to walk towards it. As it got nearer to her, I realised that the driver could not see her. Just in time, I dived at Amy, grabbing her roughly in my haste. We rolled over and over under the belly of the engine, between the large back wheels and the roller, and out through the other side. The driver stopped when he saw me and shouted, 'What the bloody hell do you think you are doing?' Then he spotted Amy. I explained what had happened and I could see sweat beads forming on his brow, as they were on mine. I was shaking like a leaf and even now when I think of that incident shivers go up and down my spine. Up to this point, Amy had been completely quiet, but now she began to holler very loudly. I was sure I had hurt her when I grabbed her. I took her back to her home and gave her mother a very stern lecture about keeping an eye on her daughter.

Unfortunately, it did no good. Not long after this incident that same little girl pulled a pan of boiling water off the cooker and scalded herself. She ran screaming out of the house. Luckily I was around that day and I plunged her straight into a bath of cold water. You could have heard her shrieks of pain two streets away. My wife Margaret telephoned for an ambulance while I tried to soothe Amy. Where was her mother? You may well ask. She was asleep on the settee, having had a liquid lunch.

The paramedics praised my efforts and said that my quick action had most likely reduced the possibility of permanent scarring.

Sadly, little Amy's suffering did not stop there. One day she opened the cleaning cupboard, picked up a bottle of Parazone cleaner, which has an acid base, opened it and drank the contents. I was called in and when I found out what she had drunk I poured as much milk inside her as she could hold. Her mother was nowhere to be seen so I shouted to Margaret to telephone for an ambulance. Amy was treated at the local hospital and her life was saved once again.

A few hours later her mother knocked on our door and asked my wife if she knew Amy's whereabouts. I was not hard on her because I had been told a few days earlier that she was very ill. She died two weeks later after visiting her daughter in hospital.

God certainly moves in mysterious ways. He gave me the strength and alertness to save that little girl on three occasions. I am sure that everything happens for a purpose and I often felt like Amy's guardian angel, watching over her and making sure that no harm came to her because her mother was too ill to look after her. Maybe one day we may know all the reasons for the things that happened to Amy in her formative years, but I am sure that she went on to great things, having survived all those tragedies at such a young age.

Alertness of mind is an asset when giving evidence in court. Sir Edward du Cann, Senior, QC, was the defence lawyer in a case in which I had given evidence about an incident I had witnessed, through some trees, in Chesham Place. Sir Edward said to me, 'Officer, I'll have you know that I have been to the scene of the alleged crime and I couldn't see through the leaves on the trees.' I replied, 'With all due respect, Sir, it is now August and the offence occurred on Boxing Day when there were no leaves on the trees.' The case was halted for a conference in the Judges' Chambers with counsel for the prosecution and counsel for the defence. On their return to the courtroom, a plea of 'Guilty' was accepted.

If I hadn't been on the ball that day, the offender might have got away with the offence.

I was a member of the Gerald Road Sea Angling Club and one bright morning at about five o'clock I was making my way to the nick prior to driving to Littlehampton on the Sussex coast. I was looking forward to catching some fish for my supper.

As I neared the Station, I saw four scruffy-looking boys walking along the road towards me. I must have looked a sight to them with my wellies, sou'wester, rods and tackle, and oilskins slung over my shoulder. I asked them where they were going at that time of the morning. They told me that they were the local paperboys going to collect their bags from the shop. I put my gear on the ground and told them to think again. I knew they were lying because my son was the local paperboy and I knew all the other paperboys.

I told them I was a police officer and searched one of the boys. In his pocket I found a gold cigarette lighter, nine gold coins, and a large green gemstone. The Police Station was close to where we were standing and I could see my colleagues who were waiting to go fishing with me. I signalled them to come over and said to the young boys, 'You see the Police Station over there, start walking towards it, and if any of you run, remember, I can run faster.' Within seconds we were all inside the nick, but my day was ruined because by the time I had filled in all the appropriate forms and got the boys' parents to come to the Station, my angling colleagues had long gone – and so too had my plan to go with them and join them in a hearty supper followed by a few beers in the local pub.

The boys were searched at the Station and we found rings, watches, cigar-cutters, and coins in mint condition, enough to stock a branch of H. Samuels. The boys wanted to know how I had known they were not paperboys. I told them that it was simply due to intuition, and they believed me.

They all admitted having escaped from an approved school and that they had carried out four burglaries during that night. I took them around the area and they identified the houses they had burgled. They were charged and returned to the approved school. Unfortunately, the school allowed them a great deal of freedom and not too long afterwards they offended again.

When they appeared before Mrs Kirwin at Westminster Juvenile Court, conclusive evidence was given and I read out the antecedents of all four boys. Between them they had twenty-nine findings of guilt, and when I heard the Magistrate give them all conditional discharges and order them to be returned to the approved school I was, to put it mildly, disgusted.

To think that I had lost the money I had paid for my fishing trip and the fish supper that was to follow! Was it worth it, I wondered.

There were many times when I was a policeman when I could have sat down and cried. Instead, I had to take control of the situation and appear to be cold and unfeeling. It was the only way I could cope and some incidents were harder to come to terms with than others.

For example, early one morning I answered an emergency call and rushed round to Glastonbury House, a block of flats off Buckingham Palace Road, where a member of the public pointed out the body of a woman lying on the pavement. Judging from the state she was in, it was clear that she had jumped from a great height. (I later learnt that she had jumped from the 19th floor.) The impact of her fall had broken the flagstones and created a dent in the pavement. I checked to see if she was in fact dead, which seemed almost unnecessary in her case but it had to be done in case a thread of life was present. Apparently, the woman, whose husband had died recently, had been visiting a friend who lived in the block of flats and whilst her friend was making a cup of tea, she went out onto the balcony and jumped.

Clearly, the poor woman was one of the many Londoners who, for whatever reason, think that no one cares about them.

The following day I was called to a florist's in Belgrave Road. On my arrival I saw a young girl wearing an apron and with a pair of scissors hanging from her waist belt. A man who introduced himself as the Manager of the shop told me he wanted the girl arrested for stealing the apron, the scissors, and a ball of ribbon. The girl burst into tears and told me she had given in her notice to leave and the Manager had gone stark raving mad when she had asked him for the holiday pay that was due to her.

I took them to the Police Station where they both made statements. The girl was charged with theft and her tears turned to hysteria when she was charged. In an effort to offer her some comfort, I said, 'Don't worry, everything will be okay. We'll clear this up and you will be free to go.'

The following day we went to Court and the Manager went into the witness box and gave his evidence. He told the Magistrate that the public must take a stand against crime, otherwise people will get away with murder. After I had given my evidence, I told the Magistrate, Mr

Barraclough, what the young girl had told me about the Manager not giving her any holiday or holiday pay in lieu, and suggested that the only reason he had made the accusation was because he did not want to pay her the money. I added that the girl had not in fact stolen the ribbon, the scissors, or the apron because they had been given to her for use at work. I concluded by telling him that I had brought the case to court because the Manager had insisted on charging the girl and I had thought it would be best for the Court to decide the matter.

After considering the evidence, the Magistrate gave the girl an absolute discharge and ordered the Manager to pay court costs of £15. He also ordered him to give the young lady her holiday pay and to reimburse her for the costs of having to appear in court. The Manager paid her there and then.

In fact, the Magistrate had no power to make the Manager pay the girl any holiday money but the Manager was not to know that. He was sickened to the core about the matter and moaned and cursed the judicial procedure and me. I told him that because of his greed he had got his just reward. The young girl, who had been so nervous and worried about how the case would turn out, left the court a happy young lady. We had righted one wrong that day and, boy, was I happy.

Gerald Road's ground was a terrific area to work in and, day or night, we never had a dull moment. We met many famous people, including Hollywood stars such as Clint Walker. Shirley Bassey lived near me, as did the late Enoch Powell. Lulu, the singer, the Bee Gees, Max Bygraves, Julie Felix, Diana Dors, and Lord Louis Mountbatten all lived on my beat. Even Her Majesty the Queen's palace garden backed on to my beat. But all of these people had their problems from time to time.

I remember one incident when I had to go to see a man called Binstock about his car, a Rolls Royce, registration number GB 69. I knocked on the door of his house and a young lady answered. Well, my eyes nearly popped out of my head. She was wearing a pink, see-through nightie. My eyes quickly dropped down to my notebook as I said, 'Mrs Binstock?' 'No,' she replied, 'she's still in bed. Come in officer.' (This young lady was none other than the one who had run away to Gretna Green with Edward Langley back in the 1950s. She was later made a ward of Court and the case was featured in the newspapers, television and on the radio.)

Mrs Patricia Binstock them came to the door. She was a well-known film star at the time and was also the 'tele-bird' for the *Daily Mirror*. I was amazed to see that she too was wearing a blue, see-through nightie. She said, 'My husband is away but would you like to join me for breakfast?'

Well, I was far too embarrassed to join her for breakfast and I didn't know where to look. However, they persuaded me to stay for a cup of tea. Mrs Binstock directed me to a room and told me to sit down near where the fireplace would normally have been. Instead, there was an ornate pool rippling with the draught coming down the chimney. (At least, that's what I thought was causing the ripple.)

She left the room and then returned with a cup of tea and a plate of biscuits. As she handed them to me I saw something that made me fling aside the biscuits and propel myself towards the door at great speed, screaming in sheer terror. It wasn't a draught coming down the chimney that was causing the water in the pool to ripple, it was a bloody great crocodile rising to the surface! No, it didn't want my tea and biscuits, it clearly thought I looked more tasty!

The two ladies were by this time laughing like hyenas at my expense. 'I'll come back some other time,' I said, as I beat a hasty retreat out of the front door. Clean underwear time again.

Chapter Nine

PARADISE LOST AND FOUND

Still in hospital and still in agony – the doses of morphine had ceased – and still being turned from side to side. Little by little it was getting easier and not hurting quite so much. I had been lying here for over a year but watching the young nurses as they performed their daily chores was a blessing.

Four days after the operation on my back, two nurses came into the ward to give me a bath. I think they were trying to tell me something. I was lifted bodily on to a trolley and taken to a specially equipped bathroom. They undressed me, removed the tube from my back and placed me onto a hoist, which they then used to lift me up and lower me into the water. I can still remember how good it felt. They rolled me over and scrubbed my back and legs and then rolled me onto my back and washed my front. I'm going to enjoy this, I thought, but my hopes were dashed when I was given a soapy flannel and told to do the rest myself. After some time they hoisted me out of the bath, dried me and dressed me in clean pyjamas.

I had just been manoeuvred into a comfortable position and was feeling warm and dry when a nurse came over and asked, 'Have you been, Mr Beard?' I replied that I hadn't. Too late, I noticed that she was wearing rubber gloves and I soon found out where that bloody big tablet was going. It wasn't long before I had 'been' and was feeling nice and comfortable again. I sank back into thinking about the great life I'd had before being savagely chopped down.

My thoughts and memories were worth more than gold to me in those terrible days. They made me laugh and they made me sad. I didn't know at the time that I'd be spending the next two years in hospital. It was probably just as well. I tried to remain positive, especially when I saw children and old people in the hospital who were in great pain or were without a hope of getting better. So who was I to complain?

My mind went back to an old lady who frequented our section and who always carried several bags of paper with her wherever she went. One sunny Sunday afternoon when it was peaceful and quiet, I was walking round my beat near the Royal Albert Hall when I saw the bag lady sitting on a bench seat. As I closed in on her she got up to leave so I called out, 'Wait there, I want to talk to you.' She asked, 'What about?' I told her I needed to talk to someone, otherwise I would go mad, it was so quiet. She sat back down again and I sat down beside her. As we chatted, I noticed she had a very refined accent, which made me think she must have come from a good background. As I broached the subject, she told me her story.

She had lived in a mansion in Berkshire with her husband and son and when her husband died, her son took over as Lord of the Manor and married soon after. Unfortunately her daughter-in-law hated her and made her life a misery, so she left before her daughter-in-law could throw her out. Since then she had lived on the streets, begging and sleeping rough.

Later I checked her story and found that what she had told me was the truth. I knew her married name and when I made contact with her son, he told me that he had been searching for his mother for a long time. He was divorced and wanted to know where he could find her. I told him and when he came to the Police Station I took him to meet her. What a wonderful reunion it was. I wish all the incidents I looked into had ended like this.

I was posted one evening with Wally Hammond to Victoria Coach Station to assist PC 'Chick' Palmer in directing the coaches arriving and leaving the Station. Being on duty with Chick was difficult because he kept disappearing and we were puzzled as to where he was going. We watched him and saw him going down an entry to the rear of the Imperial Pub, so when he came out, we shot in. There we saw a pint of beer on top of the wall, so we quickly drank it and went back out again. Later, Chick went in again, so we waited until he came out and we went in. The landlord had re-filled his glass so we again emptied it for him. This went on for some time.

The following evening we were again posted with Chick but we didn't know that when we nipped down the passage to drink Chick's beer, the Sergeant was watching us. He waited for us to come out and then he went in. He must have found the beer because when he came out he was spewing all over the place. Chick must have known someone was pinching his beer because the landlord had filled the glass with washing up liquid. Chick returned and saw the Sergeant, and blamed him for all the other occasions when the beer had been drunk. Anyway, cleanliness is next to Godliness, and the Sergeant had a good clean out.

A newly-promoted Sergeant was posted to our relief. Like all new brooms, he tried to sweep clean, but he soon came down to earth with a bump. He became the Guvnor's snout and reported everything to the boss man, and his behaviour became unbearable. It so happened on a wet and cold evening that, as I was walking in Wilton Mews, I stumbled on him hiding and watching me. Realising I had 'clocked him,' he parked his bike and began walking in Wilton Crescent with me when we heard a crashing and scraping noise coming from behind us. When we turned round we could see sparks flying from behind a car. It stopped, so we hurried back to the car. The driver got out, and to our horror we saw a bike tied to the rear bumper. You've guessed it, the badly damaged bike belonged to the Sergeant. It was clear that it was tied up with standard issue string of the kind supplied to Police Stations. Which idiot did it I'll never know, but what a laugh it caused – that is, until everyone in the Station had to dig deep into our pockets to pay for the damage.

The next night the Sergeant collared me together with a police van driver and a couple of other officers and told us he would show us how to arrest people. He thought there had not been enough arrests by the officers on his relief and that the figures had to be increased. We got into the van and drove round checking all the pubs, clubs and brothels, until we reached the *White Ferry* pub at closing time. A man came staggering out; he couldn't stand and was being taken home by his friends. The Sergeant said, 'Beard, arrest that man.' I refused, telling him that the man was only drunk and that it was clear his friends were making sure that he would get home safely. (The Law requires that a drunken person should only be arrested if he is incapable of taking care of himself.) With this, the Sergeant jumped out of the van, arrested the drunken man, and bundled him into the van. The next minute all hell broke loose. People started banging on the side of the van and they began to rock it from side to side. I thought it was going to roll over. In my opinion the man should not have been arrested because there were enough people there to take him home safely and we didn't need this sort of aggravation.

Soon after we arrived back at the Station, dozens of people rushed in shouting 'We want Kelly out.' The angry mob banged on the counter, the doors and the windows and as I looked out into the street, I saw hundreds of people there. Where they had come from, the Lord only knows because they definitely hadn't been in the *White Ferry*. (They had probably been organised by Rent-a-Mob.) The Duty Inspector remonstrated with the mob and one person was allowed in to file a complaint.

The incident turned into a complete disaster and instead of working in harmony with the general public we got hate and bitterness. It undermined good relations. It is still the same today with some police officers over-reacting, sitting in cars in plain clothes ready to arrest anyone who breathes at the wrong rate, instead of getting on with good police work and arresting people who have committed rape, burglary, criminal damage and other serious crimes.

There are people being summoned for speeding and this is only to bring up the statistics, when they have failed to catch serious offenders. I believed John Stalker when he said of statistics, 'There are lies, damn lies, and statistics.'

On a wet and windy evening in 1966, I came across a disturbance in Victoria Coach Station in which a couple of Coach Inspectors were trying to hold down a West Indian drunk. He was fighting mad, stank of alcohol and his eyes rolled round and round like fruit symbols in a gaming machine – except that whey they stopped rolling, he didn't hit the jackpot. When his eyes stopped rolling they focused on me and as soon as he realised that I was a police officer he jumped to his feet. God, he was at least 7 foot tall and just as wide! I shook in my boots because he was the biggest man I had ever seen. He did not speak but I knew what he was thinking: *What the hell does this policeman think he's going to do?*

I pulled myself to my full height and in a voice of authority I told him that I was arresting him (I think!) for being drunk in a public place. And he let me!

As we walked out of the Coach Station and headed towards Gerald Road Police Station he fell on me, knocking me over, and no sooner had I regained my balance than he fell on me again. Despite his drunkenness, I could tell he was a well-educated man and when we stopped to rest, he slurred out that he was a Head Master. I believed it: he was dressed in a well-made suit, albeit a dirty one by now. He was later charged with the offence of being drunk in a public place and the following morning he appeared before the Magistrate at Bow Street and fined 15 shillings.

I thought I would never see him again but I was wrong. One day I had just come out of Gerald Road Police Station when I saw him in Elizabeth Street, very smartly dressed, with some students. He spotted me and dashed straight over and grasped my hand, shaking it violently. He introduced me to his class of students as if I was his best friend. I thought I had better keep quiet about how we had met but to my surprise he blurted out the whole story.

I was speechless when he told me he had taken an oath never to touch the 'Devil's Tea' again. Apparently, on the day I had arrested him, he had had a family rift and had gone on a bender. He explained that he was a teacher at a Seminary and that the students were training to be priests, preachers or missionaries of some kind. He broke out into a sermon about the demon drink and said I was his saviour who had put him back on the right road. (He could have done the same for me!!) As he preached his gospel, a small crowd gathered and started clapping, the students edged in closer, and at that point I saw my chance to escape. Hallelujah!

One evening I was summoned to the Inspector's office to be told that there would be an important Reception that night at the Libyan Embassy and that members of the aristocracy would be present. I was required to assist with the traffic in the area. These were words I loved to hear. I was given this sort of job many times because we had 97 diplomatic premises on our patch and on such occasions we were often invited in for refreshments.

That night was no exception and when George Brown, MP (later Lord George Brown) came out for a breath of fresh air and started chatting to me, it wasn't long before he invited me in for a drink. As I entered, a large glass was placed in my hand and immediately filled with whisky. We were then joined by an elegantly dressed lady, and as I looked up I recognised her a none other than Her Royal Highness Princess Margaret. I started to make my excuses to leave, but she said, 'No stay here, officer. Have another whisky, have another canapé.' So on hearing this, I obeyed. Well, I always obey orders, honestly.

The three of us huddled up closely together discussing the topics of the day. (My chosen subject was: *How to run a police force*.) As the night wore on, the waiters continually topped up our glasses almost as soon as we had taken a sip. I was by now drinking and eating with Lords, Ladies, and by Royal Command, I'll have you know. I soon forgot that I was on duty until I turned round and saw the waiters watching us, giving me the most awful dirty look and begrudgingly offering me a final drink of the evening. Most of the other party guests had gone – perhaps their conversation had not been as rivetting as mine.

When we downed our last drink, we went outside and George and HRH Princess Margaret slipped into their respective cars and they sped off. I staggered back to the Police Station and as I walked in my Inspector greeted me with 'Beard, where have you been until now? The party can't have lasted this long.' 'But Sir,' I replied, 'I couldn't leave until Princess Margaret had left.' This infuriated the Inspector immensely. 'Royalty at the party, why wasn't I informed?' Not bloody likely, I thought, as I made my way out of his office.

Late one night I was walking through the back streets of Kensington. I had already checked all the important buildings and had contacted the Station to report that everything was in order, so I was looking forward to a quiet night when I saw a flash of light from a doorway. I went into another street and came up to the doorway from the other side, ran in and grabbed someone who was standing at the door. I pulled him into the light and to my horror I saw that it was the Duty Inspector! He was jumping up and down after the terrible shock I had given him. When he calmed down I had a go at him before he could rollock me and told him not to creep around my beat. Off he went, somewhat sheepishly.

I bumped into PC Gerry Adley later on and he explained to me that there was a party being held in that house and the Inspector had been hanging around waiting for an invitation. So back we went and the party had just commenced in the basement. We were invited in. I can't remember why but there must have been on some pretext.

When we got inside I saw many faces from TV fame, including Wendy Craig the actress, and Monica Rose, a hostess on the Hughie Green Show. Gerry was carrying the new-fangled personal radio with him. It weighed a ton and to this day I don't know how we carried so much equipment. We took off our coats and helmets and Gerry placed his radio on the floor. We had just been given a drink when Monica Rose scooped up the radio, pressed the button and shouted, 'Hellow all you sexy coppers!' The minute the Inspector heard it on his personal radio, he was back at the house in a flash. He walked in as I was talking to Wendy Craig. He took our pocket books with the intention of signing them (a preliminary to instigating a discipline charge) but that was his downfall because the actress Petrina Binstock and her sister grabbed him and started to undress him. At that point, Gerry and I retrieved our pocket books and ran. The Inspector never mentioned the incident again, and neither did we. (Got away with it again. Like a cat, I must have had nine lives.)

The Inspector was a good man and an excellent copper. He loved a joke and could take one as well. Whenever he played a joke on us we fell for it. However, when we tried to beat him at his own game, and we tried many times, he always outsmarted us. There was one incident that I particularly remember.

He instructed Don Docherty and myself to go to an address in Elizabeth Street where a party was to be held that night. We were told to assist with the traffic outside. We went to the venue and soon received an invitation. Drinks were put into our hand and Don, being a Scot, opted for the Scotsman's medicine. The party was swinging as we walked into the room where the music was coming from, but what we saw unnerved us both. Men were dancing with men and some had lipstick on. They looked at us and, would you believe it, they had been told that we were the cabaret act for the evening! Where had they got that idea? You may well ask.

Carefully we backed out of the room, put our glasses down and disappeared into the night as quickly as we could. I have never seen Don move as fast as he did that night. Outside, sitting in his car, was the Inspector who had been waiting for this moment – and we hadn't disappointed him. He could see by the look on our faces that his prank had worked perfectly. I'm sure that he still laughs about this little episode.

We often received calls from female au pairs who had been left alone in big houses in Belgravia whilst the owners were away either on holiday or taking a weekend break. On one such evening I received a call over the new radio to go to an address where a girl had reported seeing an intruder standing in the back garden and looking in through the window. There was a snowstorm that night with about two inches of snow on the ground.

I arrived at the house at the same time as PC Bowen. We knocked on the door and a young girl answered. 'Oh, two of you,' she said. She was a Swedish girl, very pretty, and she was wearing only a housecoat. As she stood at the door the housecoat flew open. She was wearing nothing underneath.

PC Bowen and I were invited in and she repeated that a man had been lurking in the garden. She showed us the window he had allegedly peeped through. I went outside into the snow, shone my torch around and found no footprints anywhere, so I went back in and told Bowen that there was no evidence to support the allegation. I formed the view that she wanted company for the night and she was lonely in the big house. As we stood talking there was a knock on the door; it was our old friend the Inspector who said he would take charge. We left him to close the file on the case and we admired his dedication to duty because he worked very, very hard on this enquiry.

We learnt later that he didn't leave the house until the following morning and I saw him making further calls there for a few mornings after. (Another satisfied customer.)

I remember a time when I was patrolling my beat round Victoria Station and was met by the Inspector to do a vice patrol looking for male and female prostitutes soliciting. In the case of male prostitutes we were never allowed to do these patrols when Parliament was sitting. I wonder why?

We knew all the girls who were on the game as they had been arrested many times. Some were vulgar, unkempt undesirables. On one occasion I saw a well-dressed city gent walking out of the Station with a prostitute who was very dirty. Her clothes were torn and she was clinging onto his arm. I cringe to think of these men going home and getting into bed with their wives after being with whores.

This particular evening we saw a Jaguar being driven by a lovely girl who kept stopping and talking to men. I asked one man what she had said to him. He told me she had invited him into the car for sex, so the Inspector told me to arrest her, which I did. I eventually found out that she was married to an influential man who lived in the area. She was a bored housewife and had found a thrill in soliciting men for sex and getting paid for it and enjoyed doing it in her husband's car.

Which reminds me of the story of the man who sent his wife out on the game because they had no money. She returned later in the evening and he asked, 'How much have you earned, love?' She replied, 'Ninety-nine pence.' He then said, 'Who's done you for a penny?' and she answered, 'All of them.'

Such is life.

One night I arrived for work early so I went into the Communications Room for a chat and a cuppa. Whilst I was in there, the telephone rang. I answered it and a very anxious-sounding lady who was obviously in a panic said, 'Please come quick, my husband is beating a man up in Wilton Road' She explained that the man had sexually assaulted their nine-year old daughter. Her husband had gone looking for him and found him and he was now knocking the daylights out of him. I continued drinking my tea when the telephone rang again. It was the same woman, again pleading for a police officer. The Inspector seemed to be aware of the situation and he said, 'Finish your tea and go down later.' Ten minutes passed and she rang again; 'If you don't come quick my husband will kill him.' So away we went in the van.

As we rounded the corner we saw the man hiding in Woolworth's doorway. We put him in the van and took him to the nick, where he was charged. The man was placed on the sex offenders' record and in fact he was subsequently arrested for other similar offences.

We later learnt that the family had the satisfaction of seeing justice done and we didn't have to arrest an irate father for assault.

A couple of days later two incidents occurred on the same night, both of which were quite amusing.

I was on patrol with Don Docherty and as we neared an alleyway alongside a big house we thought we'd have a quick look in and check the property. Don said, 'Did you see that? There's somebody in that tree.' I went up to the tree and saw a man in the lower branches. I dragged him out of the tree onto the ground. We went round to the back of the house and we could see a light on in the basement so Don went up to the window and came back and told me to take a look. I went to the window and saw the television was on – nothing strange about that, I thought. Don told me to take another look, so I went back and then I saw her. Lying naked on a rug was a young girl watching television, and the reason why I hadn't seen her the first time was that she was exactly the same colour as the rug.

We knocked on the door and told her to close the curtains and to lock the gate, which she did, but not in the nude. The man in the tree was duly arrested, but amazingly the girl told us that she knew the man was in the tree. She said, 'He's up that tree every night.' Well, there's a thing!

The second incident that night took place whilst we were in Belgravia. A taxi drew up to the kerb and out got a gorgeous young lady who requested the driver to assist her elderly husband out of the cab and into the house. The driver did so and left, and that was that. Or so we thought.

A man emerged from the house next door and waited until the young lady came back out and ran straight into his arms. They kissed and cuddled and then went into his flat. As they disappeared, another taxi drew up and a gorgeous looking girl got out and went into the old man's house.

We continued round our beat and came back by the same route (how could we resist seeing the next instalment?) We saw another taxi draw up at the old man's house and his young visitor came out of the house, got into the taxi, and left. Five minutes later his young wife came out of her boyfriend's flat and entered her own house. Well, it was obvious that she had thought her husband was happily tucked up in bed having a good night's sleep – which was partly true, he had a good night but not asleep – and he must also have thought that his wife was having a good night.

It had been an eventful night on the beat, but there was more to come. Later that dawn, at about five o'clock as walked through Belgravia, we heard a woman's voice call out, 'Hello, darling.' I looked up and saw a woman standing on the balcony of a house, drinking coffee. She held the coffee cup up and waved and when I looked again I saw that it was none other than Marlene Deitrich. She was always there at that time in her dressing gown with a pot of coffee. Marlene always made a point of exchanging a few words with the officer on the beat – a great actress and a lovely lady.

My radio crackled and announced my name and number. 'Go to (an address) in Wilton Crescent, dead body.' Coppers hate to hear this type of call over the radio. Anyway, away I went and dealt with the situation – doctor summoned, doctor attended, body removed, place secured, left. Some members of the dead man's family arrived and searched the address. Then they attended the Police Station and accused me of stealing £900 from the dead body! I was suspended from duty whilst enquiries were made and I was sent home to kick my heels.

A senior officer went to the house and saw that it had been ransacked. He was disgusted to think that one of his officers had been accused of doing it. The dead man's daughter arrived while he was there and told him that her husband had ransacked the house to look for the old man's insurance and the missing £900 that he had drawn out of the bank the morning he died. Then came the crunch – she also stated that they knew where the £900 was. She told the senior officer that when the old man drew out his money he went round paying off all his debts, which added up to nearly £900. When the son-in-law arrived on the scene he was given a good talking to for not telling us what he had done.

I was immediately reinstated – but with no apologies, nothing. It certainly knocks the stuffing out of you when this sort of thing happens.

The next day, I was plodding along Eccleston Street and as I crossed over the road to the post office I saw a lady come out and approach her car. I knew she wouldn't be able to get out because when she had parked she had driven too close to the car in front; and then someone had parked too close to the rear of her car. As I watched her, she got into her car, started the engine, and reversed it into the car behind - Bang! She then drove forward and hit the car in front – Bang! She again reversed into the car behind her – Bang! By now she had moved both cars about two inches. She did this about eleven times.

I'd seen enough so I went up to the driver's door, knocked on the window and told the woman to switch off the engine. I said, 'Madam, you've just had eleven accidents with two cars and damaged the rear bumper of one and the front bumper on the other.' 'Don't be ridiculous, officer,' she replied, 'that's not an accident, that's what bumpers are for.' Well, what do you say to that? I chuckled under my breath, but I had two accidents to report while she 'popped orf' to her little afternoon cocktail party and cucumber sandwiches. I can understand why policemen aren't issued with guns.

I was called to Chelsea Barracks by the Catering Sergeant to have what turned out to be a really arresting time. I met the Sergeant in the Mess and as he poured out a couple of drinks he told me that someone had been stealing whisky, rum and brandy from the Mess. He had narrowed it down to night time and had kept a watch on the premises but he hadn't been able to find out how the thefts had been carried out. I agreed to do a few nights observation, finished my drink, and left.

The first night I saw nothing amiss, only the usual lorry collecting the cookhouse garbage at the rear of the kitchens, for pigswill; no other vehicles entered the barracks that night.

On the second night I hid under a box where no one could see me. At about 2am I saw a scruffy-looking individual walk behind the bar in the Mess, pick up two bottles of scotch and put them on the bar whilst he poured himself a drink from the optics. He moaned, 'Where's the bloody ice?' He then swallowed his drink, picked up the two bottles and left. (He was the night duty pigswill collector at all the restaurants in Soho and the West End, including the Chelsea Barracks.)

I followed and saw him drive his lorry into the back yard where the kitchens were. He threw the bottles into the bins on the back of his lorry. *Plonk,* they went, into one of the bins that were full of slops that he had collected from other kitchens. As he got into the cab I grabbed him. He seemed to jump about four feet into the air and on his way down he caught a glimpse of my warrant card. 'I've just seen you nick two bottles of scotch and a glass of scotch. What have you to say for yourself?' I said. To which he replied, 'Prove it.' I said that I would.

There were two dozen bins on the back of his lorry which was covered with a canvas sheet, but it didn't hide the disgusting smell. There were bins, bins and more bins full of a disgusting stinking mess – and I had a prisoner to match. His trousers and jumper had gunge on them two years old and they were shiny with filth. The cab was the same and they both smelled like they had been dragged through a cesspit.

Anyway, I climbed into the lorry – I didn't know which bin he'd thrown the bottles into – and saw that every bin was full to the brim. I was wearing decent clothes and I could see him laughing at me so I pushed his face near the top of the nearest bin. 'I'm not going to prove it, YOU ARE,' I said as I thrust his arm into the horrible mess, 'and you are going to search each and every bin until we find the booze.'

I found an empty bin and made him tip the contents of one of the other bins slowly into it. Good gracious, I thought, how did that ham get in there, as I saw a large ham in the bottom of the bin he was emptying. It was wrapped in plastic covering to protect it. I asked him where he had obtained the ham and he replied, 'The Savoy Hotel. Every week the chef leaves two hams out, one for him and one for me. He leaves his car keys on the front tyre of his car and all I have to do is open his car and take the ham he has left for me. You are the first copper to stop me and search me. Every copper gets one whiff and off they go at great speed.' A perfect set up.

He carried on pouring garbage from one bin to another until we found not only the whisky bottles but bottles of brandy, rum, gin, sides of bacon, more hams, catering tins of food, and so on. The man was a real 'collector'.

The lorry was taken to Gerald Road where it was parked. None of the other lads would go near it so I had to drive it myself. The prisoner was put in a cell whilst enquiries were made and half the chefs in the West End were arrested and brought in. During the night there were complaints from the neighbours about the smell emanating from the Police Station into the street. Lady St Just, who lived next door to the Station, rang to complain and said, 'We can't have this smell in Belgravia, it's just not on, old boy.' The lorry was then removed to the coach station.

We sorted out all the tins of pork, beef, Spam, the side of bacon, etc., and put them in front of each person who had either stolen or unlawfully handled them. We charged the driver and bailed him to appear at Bow Street Magistrates Court, and then released him, which reduced the smell a little. The chef of the Savoy admitted stealing the whole pig, half for himself and half for the pig man, he was charged, bailed, and released. And so it went on.

We dealt with thirteen prisoners that night until the Station Officer told us all to go home and have a bath, have some breakfast and be back by 9am sharp. By 9am, all the prisoners had cleaned themselves up and the nasty smell had died away.

Bow Street Magistrates Court was full that morning and our friend the pig man played his ace card – he came to court in his working clothes. Everyone in the Court got a whiff of him and complaints were banded about everywhere so the case was brought forward. Heavy fines were imposed but there was no prison sentence for the pig man because we would have had to have kept him inside. As someone pointed out, the case stank! My wife complained about the state of my clothes and threw them in the dustbin.

This case brought to mind another, also stinking but not quite so badly, which concerned an old tramp who was known to many London police officers and even the Essex County Force. Dennis Rough was his name, and Dennis walked everywhere. He never rode on a train or bus but always walked from somewhere in the Fulham area to Southend in Essex – and then he walked all the way back. He did this twenty or more times a year. We all knew he did it, but no one bothered to find out why.

That is, until one day when I stopped him and asked him where was going. I could smell him but thought, 'Now I've started, I'll finish.' He replied, 'Southend; I go every two weeks.' I asked him what he had in his pockets and put my hand in and brought out a handful of jewellery. There were rings worth up to £4,000 and an international wristwatch amongst other things. I asked him where he had obtained them but he refused to tell me. After asking him some more questions, which he also refused to answer, I arrested him and took him to Chelsea Police Station. (I had stopped him on their patch.)

Whilst being questioned at the nick, he broke down and told us that he was the main carrier of a lot of property that had been stolen in London. In fact, he had been a carrier for twenty years and had taken it to wherever the villains wanted it delivered. No one had thought to stop Dennis until that day, but I got my come-uppance when I started to scratch and had to be deloused and fumigated. Notwithstanding, I had put a stop to Dennis's little game.

Chapter Ten

A KNIGHT IN SHINING ARMOUR – GONE DULL

I was now well into my second year on division.

I was taking a break in the canteen when Sergeant Plumbley came in and asked me to go to Buckingham Palace Road to remove a man who was drunk on a No.11 bus. When I arrived, the driver and conductor were standing on the footway beside the bus. The conductor told me that the drunk was on the top deck so up I went. When I reached the top of the stairs I saw a disgusting sight. There was vomit everywhere and it stank to high heaven. The smell was overpowering and I heaved. A man holding his head in his hands was leaning over the seat in front. There was sick all over the seat.

I told him to get off the bus. He looked up and then buried his head in his hands again, completely ignoring me. I lifted him to his feet and as I did so he took a wild swing at me. Fortunately, he was way off target but I ducked nonetheless and took hold of his arm as it went past my head. I tried to march him to the exit, which was not an easy thing to do because he continued to throw punch after punch at me. I also had very sore shins where he was putting the boot in.

When we reached the top of the stairs he lunged forward and we both went down, collapsing in a heap at the foot of the stairs with me underneath. I got him to the footway and as I did so he gave me a beautiful uppercut, followed by several punches to my head. The law of averages says that some punches will connect – and some of them did.

Without giving me any help or even a thank you, the driver got into his cab and drove off like the clappers. I was now left with the drunk who was about six feet tall and built like an outhouse. When his fist connected with my body, it certainly hurt. The onlookers stood by as he belted me and he was waving his arms around like an out of control windmill. He fell over and I pulled him up, only for the same thing to be repeated over and over as we inched our way towards the Police Station.

As we reached the block of married quarters where I lived – which was only a short distance from the Police Station – I saw the senior officer in charge of Gerald Road Police Station who was on his way home. He and his family also lived in these quarters. We were all three now at the underground garage entrance to the quarters and I was feeling tired and weak. The drunk gave me another left hook that Henry Cooper would have been proud of so I called out to my Commander for help. I shouted a second time and then when I looked round I saw him running down into the underground garages until he was out of sight. He had run away!

I cursed him under my breath and thought: when it comes to real policing there are some gutless uniform-carriers about. God, I felt disillusioned! I would never like to fight a battle with a colleague like that at my side. He had run away in the face of our common enemy – and the drunk was not even armed! I'd seen more courage in a Tom and Jerry cartoon.

Anyway, I got the prisoner to the nick unaided and he appeared at Court the next day. Mr Barraclough, the Magistrate, was sitting on the bench that day. He was getting to know me by now and before I could give my evidence he fined the prisoner £15 with £2 costs. After the case, the prisoner disappeared into the crowd without remembering what he had done. All the costs of that day were once again borne by the taxpayer.

My dealings with that senior officer did not end there. I was walking around Pimlico when I noticed a young lad riding a motorcycle. I knew him to be the senior officer's son because he and my son had played together from time to time. I also knew the lad was not old enough to drive a motor vehicle. I stopped and questioned him and he told me that the motorcycle belonged to his friend, so I pushed the motorcycle back to his friend's house. I asked his friend if he had given the other lad permission to ride his motorcycle. He hadn't, so I arrested young Mr X for taking and driving away a motor vehicle without the owner's consent.

I took them both to the nick and took a statement from the owner and just as I was seeing him off the premises, in walked the Duty Inspector who asked why the senior officer's son was in the nick. When I explained, he turned to the boy and said, 'Go on, off you go home.' I was dumbfounded and simply stared at him. He said, 'Never, never arrest a senior officer's son, even for crime. How far do you think you will get in the Job if you do things like that?' I asked him, 'If he had been my son, would you have reacted in the same way?' He mumbled something about insubordination and walked away. I was disillusioned once again, but at least I knew my sons had more sense than to do something stupid like that.

We were on van patrol one night when we answered an emergency call to go to Sloane Street where a doctor had smashed a shop window and was fighting in the street. The driver switched on the blue light and the horn and just as we were about to overtake a 'Findus Fish' van it turned right and, bang, we ran straight into its side, ripping it open like a sardine tin. I hit the windscreen, shattering it on impact, and flew into the hole in the side of the fish van, ending up covered from head to toe in fish! Blood spurted out of my forehead and shot about three feet in front of me. I tried to stop the flow by applying pressure with my hand but a large piece of glass was sticking out of the wound.

I managed to get hold of the radio to call for urgent assistance and asked for an ambulance to be sent to Sloane Street immediately. Back came the reply, 'Where in Sloane Street?' I was angry because Sloane Street is only half a mile long and it runs straight from end to end. Any ambulance driver couldn't fail to see the accident! I replied, 'How the bloody hell should I know, I'm injured and lying inside a fish van.' I passed out and when I came to in St George's Hospital, the glass had been removed from my forehead. I was x-rayed, sewn up and bandaged, and then sent home. The following day a police car driven by Reg Butcher with horns blaring stopped outside my door and took me back to hospital. A doctor informed me that I had a fractured skull and I was detained in hospital for the next few days.

When I returned to duty, I was summoned into the Guvnor's office and reported for using bad language over the radio. At that moment, he was lucky I didn't hit him as I tried to explain to him what I had gone through on that assignment. The charge was eventually dropped.

I was soon restored to full health and one day as I as walking along Kinnerton Street, I stopped to admire a sweet little baby lying in a pram. Her mother came out and spoke to me and as she did so I noticed out of the corner of my eye that further up the street a blonde-haired lady had fallen over. When I got closer I could see that she had caught the heel of her shoe in a crack in the pavement. I helped her to her feet and assisted her to her home, which luckily for her was nearby. It was then that it struck me that the person I had been helping was none other than Diana Dors! She was very grateful for my assistance.

On another occasion, after calling at a house on an enquiry but getting no reply, I was just turning to leave when a beautiful lady came out of the house next door. We conversed briefly and then she invited me in for coffee. I thought she had an American accent and she was amazed that I didn't know who she was, so she got out a photograph of herself, signed it and passed it to me. Bloody hell, what an idiot! I wanted to join the CID and yet I hadn't recognised this beautiful actress! Her name was well known – it was Racquel Welch.

During the course of the next three months I was on protection duty with Enoch Powell. He was being given protection because he had caused a stir over race relations and it was thought his life may be in danger. Enoch and I lived not far from each other and my wife could see me from our flat as I stood outside his house. She often stopped for a chat.

I got on very well with Enoch and his family, and his wife treated me very kindly every time I did duty at the house. At the end of my three months' duty, Mrs Powell invited my wife and me to dinner. We had a wonderful evening and chatted about many things, but no one mentioned politics. Enoch and his wife seemed to enjoy the evening and the company as much as my wife and I did.

More protection duty, this time outside the Saudi Arabian Embassy. One morning as I arrived to relieve the officer who had been there since the early hours, I saw him trying to get a bullet out of its casing by hitting it on the fence with his revolver. I called him an idiot and told him I'd come back when he had blown himself up.

Later on a young girl came towards me leading a lame horse. I stopped her and lifted one of the horse's hooves and saw that all but one of the nails in its shoe had come out. The shoe spun round and when the horse took a step the nail went right up into the centre of its hoof, causing it great pain.

I held the horse's leg between mine and tried to wrench the shoe off but I couldn't budge it. I needed something to lever it off so I took out my revolver. At the sight of it, the girl let out a terrible scream, which caused people to turn to see what was afoot (*pun!*) She shouted, 'Don't shoot it, it's not mine!' The crowd was ready to lynch me, but their attitude changed when I levered the gun under the shoe. The nail came out, the shoe fell to the ground, the girl was happy, the crowd was happy, and the horse was ecstatic as it trotted back to its stable.

I was never bored; I took a great deal of interest in everything I did. I loved the job and I loved night duty because you could always depend on something happening.

I was walking through a Mews late one night when I saw a French window open on the ground floor of a large house. I thought it was strange so I went inside, flashed my torch around and saw two people in bed. They jumped up and became very angry, shouting at me to get out. When I told them it was unwise to leave the windows open, they told me it was none of my business.

I reported the incident and the following night it happened again so I reported it to the Guvnor. He told me not to go there again, so I told another officer. This other officer went in and got the same treatment from the two people so he also reported the incident.

A few nights later, someone else went into the house, and it wasn't a copper. The couple were tied up, the house was ransacked and thieves stole everything of value. The occupants called in the police who pointed out the error of their ways. This wasn't the end of the matter because when the insurance company investigated the claim they found the couple had been negligent and refused to pay their losses. The insurance companies always check with police before paying out.

Sergeant 'Sailor' Bowers was a good police officer. Before joining the police force he had been a naval diver during the war and had been responsible for many heroic exploits. He dived in some terrible weather conditions but his efforts went unrewarded.

One night, 'Sailor' got a few of us together to do road checks. The first driver I stopped was the songwriter Mark Sarne who hit the music charts with 'Come Outside'. The conversation went something like this:

'Is this your car, sir?'

'No, it isn't.'

'What is the registration number of this vehicle?'

'I don't know.'

'Come outside.'

We both realised what I'd said and burst out laughing.

The next car I stopped contained four young lads. I asked the same questions again and got more or less the same answers. I suspected they had stolen the vehicle. They caved in after further questioning and were duly arrested for stealing the car and driving without insurance and driving licence. They went to court and got their just rewards.

I was on Late Turn and strolling along Pimlico Road when I saw something shiny lying on the ground ahead of me. I picked it up and saw it was a diamond tiara. Property found in the street has to be valued so I thought I'd get this done at a nearby jeweller's. The jeweller told me that the tiara was worth £20,000 and that he knew the owner. She had just collected it after having had it repaired. A quick telephone call was made from the Station to the lady owner who visited the nick where it was restored to her. Just think, in those days you could buy a street of houses for that kind of money.

Chapter Eleven

BRING OUT YOUR DEAD

I had dealt with nine dead bodies in seven days but the tenth is one that sticks in my mind.

I was called to *The Feathers* public house in Victoria where a man had hanged himself in the toilet. The Duty Inspector arrived with two young constables and asked me to let them deal with the case for experience. The first PC wouldn't go in the pub; the second climbed the stairs to the toilet and ran out as fast as he could, so I had to go in. I climbed the stairs to the toilet, which had a very small cubicle. The man had tied a wire round his neck and around the water pipe and then hanged himself by jumping off the toilet seat.

The ambulance arrived and I borrowed a machete type knife from them. I half closed the cubicle door to give myself room to cut the man down. *Rigor mortis* had set in and he was as stiff as a board. I cut the wire with the machete and the body dropped straight down, falling upright against the door and wedging it tightly shut as if I'd put a wooden prop against it. I was trapped inside the tiny room with a man who wasn't saying anything. I tried not to panic. I felt as if I was in an upright coffin.

I tried to prise him with my foot, lifting him, pushing him, and twisting him, but he would not move. In my panic, I 'told' him to move over but for some reason he wouldn't listen. There was no sign of help from my colleagues, but I could hear them laughing their heads off at my predicament.

Panicking, I pushed the corpse to one side, but it fell back again, pinning me against the door. Then I managed to push it into the corner and I was able to open the door and squeeze through a very narrow gap.

But my friend was not to be outdone; he fell back into place, slamming the door shut again and propping it up as he had done before. At last, I was outside the cubicle – but I couldn't get back in! We were back to square one. The landlord let me smash the door off its hinges as the men arrived to take the body away.

The next challenge was to get the temporary coffin up the stairs. I told my colleagues to place the open coffin at the bottom of the stairs and then I grabbed the body and let it go. Whoosh! It slid down the stairs like a plank of wood, straight into the coffin. They slammed the lid on and before I could catch my breath the body was taken away in the van, all in five seconds flat. Got you at last, you bugger!

I later learnt that the man was 67 years old and that he had hanged himself because his wife had kicked him out of the family home.

⟫ ◐ ⟪

My two years' probationary period was coming to an end so I was sent to Hendon for two weeks to take my Final examination. I had studied long and hard, not only because I needed the job, but because I loved it. After I had sat the exam, I returned to Gerald Road refreshed and thrilled because I had passed the Final.

I thought I would ease myself back into the workload gently after the stress of the previous two weeks but my Sergeant had other ideas. I was put on two weeks' attachment to the CID under the wing of Detective Sergeant Mike O'Leary, a very experienced officer and a good man to learn from.

On my first morning with the CID, DS O'Leary told us that he had just learned of a fraud that was being perpetrated at the offices of BOAC (now British Airways). BOAC had nine new double-decker coaches that were designed to do about 21 miles to the gallon of diesel but they were only doing about 5 miles to the gallon. It was thought that the fraud was being committed at a garage in Semley Place where the coaches were refuelled. WDC Pat Coates kept observation outside the garage for some time but she saw nothing suspicious. DS O'Leary said to me, 'You live opposite the garage, what can you see from your window?' The kitchen window of my flat overlooked the garage – a perfect place for an observation. Using a pair of toy binoculars belonging to one of my sons, we could see the garage clearly. The scene was set for the following day.

In the morning I cleaned the windows so there was not a smudge on them. I then went to Boots the Chemist in Piccadilly where I saw a family friend, Mr Witty, the General Manager who let me have the use of two pairs of binoculars. DS O'Leary and I made ourselves comfortable at my kitchen window and pointed our binoculars at the garage. I could see everything that was going on in the office and I could even see the prices on the till. We sat and waited.

At last a coach drove on to the garage forecourt and its registration number was noted and written down. The coach driver drew up to the pump and I could clearly see the numbers going round on the pump register until it reached 10 gallons – and then it stopped. The driver went into the office and signed for the fuel, the attendant gave him paper money from the till and he left. This went on throughout the day until all the coaches had been filled.

During the evening we went to BOAC to retrieve the copies of the dockets that the drivers had signed and took them back to the Station where we checked them against the readings that we had already recorded. The first driver had signed for 20 gallons but he had only filled the coach with ten. They had all signed for more fuel than they had received and had also received cash in hand. It was obvious that they were all in it together. Subsequent enquiries revealed that four members of the garage staff were also in on the fraud.

By the end of the week we had all the evidence necessary to secure a conviction. I made a 48-page statement, which was short in comparison with Mike O'Leary's, and when all the dockets, the photocopies, and the final papers were collated, the pile stood seven feet high.

All twelve drivers were arrested. One driver was off sick and I went to his house with Pat McGoohan who told him he was under arrest, but just as he was giving him the official caution he stopped abruptly because the man (who was 67 years old) dropped dead on the floor.

The trial took place six months later at the Old Bailey and I spent three long days in the witness box. All the garage staff pleaded guilty and they were given prison sentences. All but three of the coach drivers were also sent to prison; the others were released on points of law, which was very frustrating. We later found out that one of the jurors had been 'nobbled' by friends of some of the coach drivers.

I received a Commissioner's Commendation. Not bad, only two years in the police force and already I had received three commendations.

After this incident, I came down to earth with a bump – literally. I was walking along South Eaton Place where new-fangled parking meters had been installed. I had only seen them in the West End at that time. A young lady I knew well came out of her house and walked towards me on the other side of the road. She always wore the shortest of mini skirts – in fact I thought her skirt was a belt – but she was able to get away with it because she had a lovely figure. She shouted 'hello' to me as she walked past and I turned round to get another glimpse, but when I turned back I walked straight into a parking meter and was left feeling bruised and dazed.

The next thing I knew, this young lady was kneeling beside me, holding my head. I saw my helmet sitting on top of the parking meter, so I thought I'd stay where I was for a few more minutes. I was enjoying having her arm around my neck. I cannot print what she said to me when she realised that I was perfectly okay, but it was worth it, she did have lovely legs.

Every year, Sergeants submit a record of each officer's work during the previous twelve months. Also recorded are his hobbies, voluntary work, etc. It was odd that on my record it was noted that I played the violin. I had never played the violin or any other musical instrument. That's how daft the system was. One advantage of the reporting system was that all the lazy men who found a cushy job in the nick had to go out and do some police work if they wanted a good report.

I was out one day with one of these idlers when we got a call to go to Lyons Corner House where we saw a man who was selling milk from a churn in a pram. The man readily admitted stealing the pram and he also admitted stealing the milk from Lyons Corner House. We returned the milk to the proprietors and then we returned the pram to its owner. The police constable with me asked, 'What do we do now?' He had over twenty years in the Job and had spent 19 of them sitting on his backside. So I did what was necessary, including making the arrest and charging the thief, who appeared at Bow Street Magistrates Court the following morning.

Just before the hearing, I discovered that the thief had escaped from Banstead Mental Hospital, so I rushed into the Court where my colleague was about to give evidence. I whispered to him to stop the case, but he didn't understand, so I jumped into the witness box myself and asked for the case to be dismissed. The Magistrate obliged. But mental or not, the thief knew what money was.

I had been on Alpha One area car for a few days when a message came over the radio to the effect that a robbery was in progress at an engineering firm in Buckingham Palace Road where the wages had been stolen. Three men with guns had held up the van delivering the wages and had taken approximately seven thousand pounds. They had escaped in a getaway car driven by the fourth member of the gang. We searched the area for the getaway car and found it in the back streets of Victoria.

CID officers arrived and when the vehicle was searched one of them found a piece of paper containing an address of an hotel in Jersey. The CID officer was immediately sent by aeroplane to Jersey. In the meantime, Jersey police were informed and observation was kept on the hotel. They did not have to wait too long for a result.

Later that day the gang arrived at the hotel with their families and no sooner had they booked in and made their way to their hotel rooms than from out of nowhere the 'boys in blue' burst in and arrested the gang members, and recaptured most of the stolen money.

I have no doubt that to this day the thieves haven't figured out how they had committed the crime and flown to Jersey, only to find that the police had arrived before them. They did get their holidays in the end – free ones at that – at one of Her Majesty's prisons.

We had a lot of fun with ambulance crews in those days and there was always plenty of friendly rivalry between the local ambulance crew and their local nick. It started merely because they were bored at times. I remember one occasion in wintertime when I'd just relieved Arthur Cailaby on a traffic duty point. It was snowing hard and Arthur had been waving his arms about, directing traffic for a couple of hours, and the back of his coat was covered with snow. He stood at the side of Grosvenor Gardens getting rid of the snow and trying to get warm again. I had my back to the wind and was directing traffic when an ambulance came up behind me. As it slowed down, the driver picked up a washing up bottle filled with water and squirted it down the back of my neck. It was freezing cold. The crew laughed their heads off and then were gone in a flash.

All traffic stopped, pedestrians who had witnessed the incident clapped and cheered, and drivers were cheering from their vehicles – so I did the courteous thing and bowed. But I was saturated. Just as I was trying to dry myself off, Inspector Geoff Rush came by. He could not understand why all the traffic had stopped or what the hullabaloo was all about. I told him a lot of snow had gone down my neck.

I vowed not to forget this incident so during my next tour of night duty (as plain clothes observer on the area car) I went to the stables at Rochester Row Police Station and collected three bags of horse manure. From there I went straight to the Ambulance Station but there was nobody in the office. I even checked the loos but there was no one there, so I took the three bags of manure and emptied them on the desk and all around the office.

As I made my way to the door I smiled to myself, happy at the thought of what I had done, but just as I got out of the door buckets of water came lashing down on me from the roof, completely drenching me – and my new coat. No wonder no one was in the office, they were all on the roof, the swines.

I went home and changed but I was soon back. I got a jack and a wheel brace and went to their car park, jacked up all the cars, and left. We returned at 6am to see the fun. Most of the cars were without wheels, some had only two, and they were all on bricks. What fun it was to see them trying to sort out which wheel fitted which car. The tyres were all in a heap. We blew the car horn, and they cursed us. I knew they'd get their own back so we would have to be on our guard.

Applications were called for from uniform PCs who wished to join the Criminal Investigation Department. This was what I wanted to do so I typed out my application and included all the information about the crime work I had done. I thought that the three awards I had received would stand me in good stead and I was thrilled to receive a notice to attend an interview. In the meantime, I carried on with my normal duties and the next incident was very nearly my downfall.

Someone had thrown a bomb at the Spanish Embassy and blown some of it away. The following evening I found myself at the Embassy on guard duty. After a while the Ambassador invited me into the kitchen where some food and tea had been laid on. I didn't need asking twice. The timing was dreadful, because a minute later who should come along but Inspector Rush. He was livid when he found no one guarding the Embassy and he waited outside the front door for me to return to my post. When I did so he yelled at me, 'You're going to be on a charge, Beard, and that will put paid to your ideas about joining the CID.' Then he went on his way, leaving me hoping that when he cooled down he would forget about putting me on a discipline report.

A few minutes after he had gone, there was a loud crash as two cars collided with each other outside the Embassy. I dashed over and what a mess met my eye. One man had been thrown clear of his vehicle and had sustained massive head injuries. At first I thought he was dead but I saw him twitch slightly and decided to attempt to resuscitate him. I managed to get him breathing again and monitored him until an ambulance crew arrived. The paramedics swiftly took him to hospital. Later I heard that my actions had saved the man's life and he is still alive today and in good health.

It was a humbling experience bringing this chap back from the throes of death and although I was exhausted that night I certainly felt that I had done a good night's work.

The following day, I was posted to the Hyde Park Hotel to guard Sir Edmund Hilary, the first person to reach the summit of Mount Everest. By coincidence, Chay Blyth and John Ridgeway, who had rowed the Atlantic in ER2, were also staying at the hotel. I asked them for their autographs – for my sons, of course.

During this tour of duty, I was free to roam about so when it got dark I found a corner where I could have a crafty smoke. However, as I lit my cigarette the Duty Inspector arrived, so I curled up my fingers with the cigarette inside them and held my hand up the sleeve of my topcoat – as many officers have done before me, and probably still do today – to conceal the evidence. Unfortunately, the Inspector was in a chatty mood and spoke to me at length. I felt sure that the ciggy was getting near the end because I could feel the heat from it and I was more than glad when he said, 'You can drop that cigarette now before you set yourself alight.' Then he walked off without saying another word.

I've picked up pieces of dead bodies from an air crash in Lincolnshire, I've pulled dead bodies from a lake near Borehamwood, from burning houses, from vehicles, and from between vehicles. I've attended scenes where hangings, strangulations, and murders have taken place, and I have removed bodies from a bin and from a dustcart. I have also been to post mortems. But nothing upset me as much as the occasion when a man threw himself at a train, not under it, but at it. The train didn't surrender, it mangled him and threw the bits to the four winds over a distance of half a mile. The train was in a mess, the lines were in a mess, and it was a terrible job for those who had to clear away the debris. I felt sorry for the relatives because there was no body to bury, just the pieces. Then there was the job of telling the relatives. There is no easy way to tell them that their loved ones are dead. I have had to do this terrible job many times and it was never a task that I looked forward to.

I remember one day when I had to tell a relative about an unexpected death. I knocked on the door and a lady answered. I asked if I could come in and wondered how to find the right words to tell her what had happened. Should I come straight out with it or what? I said, 'Please sit down, your husband has been hit by a train.' Her reaction was totally unexpected – she laughed. 'He's been threatening to kill himself for ages,' she said, 'let me make you a cup of tea.'

Life is cheap to some people, they don't seem to care how they die, but throwing oneself in front of a train seems to be such a selfish act. The traumatic effect on train drivers when this type of incident occurs is enormous and some train drivers never drive again.

One evening I was called to a disturbance in Grosvenor Mews. I knocked on the door and a woman answered. I recognised her and asked her was the problem was. She invited me in and said, 'This man is trespassing and I want him out.' The man she was referring to was in fact her husband. She showed me a court order which stated that he was not allowed on the premises, so I turned to him and said, 'You've heard what she said, now move.' With this, he sheepishly left the house. I turned to the woman and asked her for her name and address – I knew it but I had to ask. She replied, 'Mrs Miller.' I said, 'Pardon?' She said, 'All right, my name is Christine Keeler.' There was another woman present. I recognised her face from newspaper photographs. She was Mandy Rice-Davies.

I left the premises and hung around outside to ensure that the man didn't come back, but I was soon moved on by Detective Superintendent 'Nipper' Read who was keeping undercover observation on *The Grenadier* public house which was used by the Kray twins and they were inside the pub that evening. I had often seen them coming and going as I walked my beat and I always made a note of their movements for the information of the Collator.

As a means of earning extra money, I often volunteered for crowd control duty at Chelsea Football Ground, especially when Chelsea were playing Manchester United. The latter were usually the victors, which upset some of the Chelsea fans who would attend the game with the intention of causing trouble so the Chief Inspector in charge of policing the game handpicked a few of us to search them before they entered the ground.

Within about ten minutes flat we had enough arms to start a war. One officer was rushed to hospital after having put his hand in one man's pocket. His fingers had been cut to ribbons on some penny coins which had been sharpened and honed to a sharp edge round the rim. We had no doubt that the man responsible had intended to throw the coins at the opposition. The stupid individual was arrested and dealt with accordingly.

I arrested one boy who had a machete concealed down one leg of his trousers. Other youngsters had Stanley knives, flick knives, gravity knives, ball bearings, nuts and bolts, spikes, knuckle-dusters and all sorts of manufactured and homemade weapons. Some had umbrellas with the tips sharpened to a point with the intention of being used to stab opposition supporters. We also found lead piping and swordsticks; the list was endless. The word soon got around about the search so some youngsters threw their weapons over the perimeter wall and collected them when they got inside the ground. However, we had anticipated them so we put the word around that searches would be carried out as the fans were leaving the ground. After they had left we found dustbins full of weapons.

All the time I was carrying out searches, a press photographer followed me wherever I went. Unfortunately, his camera was accidentally knocked out of his hands and trodden on by a supporter.

By the end of the day, we had a van full of weapons and vans full of the owners of the weapons. The offenders were all charged and to avoid retaliation against the other supporters they were detained until two hours after the match had ended.

I remember that at one of the matches I instinctively caught a ball that had been kicked by Bobby Charlton. I wished I hadn't because it felt as if it had been hit at 100 miles an hour. So I now know what goalkeepers around the world must feel when they stop a well-struck ball aimed straight at them. You'll be pleased to know that Bobby Charlton was not arrested for possessing an offensive weapon.

After one football match, I spotted an affray in which two or three young-sters were fighting and six or seven others were encircling them. I stepped into the circle and stopped the fight. Finding myself surrounded, I saw the flash of knives and then someone said, 'Let's get this copper.' Without hesitation, I drew my truncheon, held it by the strap, and spun around as fast as I could a few times, hitting as many of the lads as possible. The two with the knives were on the ground but the others backed off and ran away. I told the two to stay put and swiftly took their knives from them and arrested them. It wasn't until afterwards that I realised how nasty it could have been. After a few sweats and shakes, I managed to get back to normal.

Police officers should never go into situations like that alone, but we never learn and some officers have lost their lives in such circumstances. Sadly, the one man who sticks in my mind is PC Keith Blakelock who was later murdered during the riots at Broadwater Farm in Tottenham.

Chapter Twelve

ONLY AN ACCIDENT

According to the dictionary, an accident is an occurrence happening by chance, a mishap, a casualty or a contingency. Well, I have often wished that I hadn't been sent to the scene of an accident, but when an order is given you have to act on it.

Do you remember when the entertainer Jimmy Saville appeared on TV instructing us all to belt up? He mentioned that statistics showed that 95% of accidents in motorcars happen within 10 miles from home. Over 90% of motorists don't go more than ten miles from home in the first place. Most London car owners are simply using their cars for shopping, school runs and the like.

One traffic accident happened at Grosvenor Gardens at the junction with Buckingham Palace Road where two cars came into contact at the traffic lights. When I got there some ten minutes later, traffic was piling up by the minute and motorists were getting irate, honking their horns and shouting at each other.

I asked the driver of one wreck what had happened and he replied, 'Ask this idiot here, he drove straight through a red light and hit me.' I turned to the other driver, an Algerian, who said in broken English, 'The light was blue. When I saw the blue light, I drove straight across and he hit me.' I assured him that we did not have blue traffic lights in Britain and asked him what colour the traffic lights were at that moment. He replied, 'They are still blue.' The lights were in fact showing red, and I told him so. Road rage continued until more officers arrived to assist me with clearing up the mess. This case went to court and when I gave my evidence, the Court was in uproar when I said, 'The red lights were blue.'

The next metal entanglement happened whilst I was on night duty. When I arrived I saw that two cars had crashed head-on in a one-way street. One driver said, 'I didn't see him until he was out of sight.' I wondered what I had got myself into and turned to the other driver, who said, 'It shouldn't have happened, because I shouldn't be here.' *(Beam me up Scotty, I thought to myself— we have Kling-ons on the starboard bow.)*

I got to the crux of the matter when one of the occupants told me, 'We were following each other to a party.' I asked, 'Now how the hell did you hit each other head-on if you were following each other?' 'Well officer,' he replied, 'he took a wrong turn so we went around the block to head him off. We failed to see him and we crashed.' In true training school fashion I shouted to the gathered crowd, 'Did anyone else see what happened?' I wished I hadn't because one man answered, 'Yes, I did.' He stepped out of the group of by-standers and said, 'This car came up here, the other came from that end of the Street and they hit head-on but it happened before I got here.' (This is why lawyers attend universities; so that they can introduce new case law, as necessary.) When the evidence was given at court, the Clerk of the Court held his head in his hands trying to suppress his laughter and the Magistrate had a job to keep a straight face. He eventually just fined both drivers. I wonder what would have happened if he had heard what the witness had to say!

Which brings to mind an accident that occurred on a traffic island. When I arrived at the scene I saw a mini motorcar in the middle of the island with four occupants inside and alongside this car was the biggest lump of granite I had ever seen.

The granite was a kerbstone, not a manufactured kerbstone, but one hewn out of solid rock. It must have weighed three hundredweight and when I looked back up the road about 100 yards I saw a hole where it had been. Apparently the mini was travelling at excessive speed, it hit the kerb, ripped out the chunk of granite and dragged it down the road to the middle of the island where it came to rest. The occupants of the mini were of foreign origin and were protected by Diplomatic Privilege. They had all been drinking. The driver's legs and feet were crushed by the foot pedals and I couldn't move them. A flame was coming from under the bonnet but when I checked it out, it was not life threatening at that very moment, though I knew I had to keep an eye on it.

The front seat passenger was unhurt and got out of the vehicle to help. There were two beautiful young ladies in the back. I helped one of them out of the car but because she had only minor injuries I told the other passenger to look after her. The third passenger, who I was told later was a Princess, appeared to have injured her back. As I gently eased her out of the vehicle she screamed in agony. I laid her on the ground on my coat then wrapped it around her.

I tried to put the flame out under the car until the fire brigade arrived. An ambulance arrived at the same time and together they cut the driver free; a second ambulance arrived and carted him off to the hospital. The Princess's injuries were serious and she had to be put in a straight splint to protect her head and back before she could be moved; then at last all were taken to hospital.

The vehicle was removed, but the lump of granite stayed where it was, I wasn't moving that. The Princess had a broken hip and serious back injuries. She sent a message for me to visit her in the hospital and I was told that she had a gift for me, but I never went because I had only been doing my job and to save a life was payment enough.

I was walking along Buckingham Palace Road when I saw a crowd of people standing round a double-decker bus. When I arrived I saw two small legs sticking out between the double back wheels. I crawled under the bus and saw a young boy who was unable to move. Thankfully he was still alive so I came back out, realizing that the situation was not looking good and that we had to get him out immediately.

I know that buses can tilt at a dangerous angle before they overturn so I got the assembled crowd to lift the rear nearside of the bus until it began to tilt. I was already down on the ground and gave the boy's legs a good tug. Out he came from between the wheels and the bus bounced back on to the ground.

I'd pushed this lad onto the footway and by the time I got to my feet he had run off as fast as his legs could carry him. I thought he must have been injured so I checked all nearby hospitals, without success. I wondered what to report in the Personal Injury Accident Report because there had been no opportunity to find out if the boy had been injured. The incident puzzles me to this day.

One Sunday two of us were on patrol in the van when we came across an accident in which a car had hit a parked car and the driver had decamped. The car he had hit belonged to Avis Car Hire, so we had it towed back to their garage where it was handed over to a woman agent who searched the vehicle and removed the contents. We resumed our patrol and thought no more about the matter.

The following day we were called into the office and the Inspector asked, 'What did you do with the contents from the Avis Car yesterday?' We didn't know anything about the contents of the car. Apparently the hirer of the Avis car had reported that articles had gone missing from the vehicle. We were the suspects and so we were suspended from duty, until contact could be made with the Avis Representative. When she came back after two weeks' leave in Spain, the Investigating Officer questioned her. She told him that she had removed the articles in question and put them in her locker for safekeeping.

The police constable who had been suspected along with me told the Guvnor what he thought of the job and resigned. I decided to await the outcome of the investigation because I only had two years' service and I had a family to keep. It takes the biscuit when you're not trusted to do the job you love.

The law sometimes works for the villain of the piece and sometimes to the advantage of the victim. I agreed with the decision in the following case.

I was again in the area car when we heard over the radio that a car was being chased along the Ml from the North of England. We didn't take much notice because the vehicle was a long way from us, but we became interested once it entered the Metropolitan Police area at Edgware and continued along the Edgware Road.

We then positioned ourselves at Hyde Park Corner and waited. It was not long before the vehicle appeared and we took over the chase along

Grosvenor Place, Chester Street, Belgrave Square, into Chesham Place, and then right into Lowndes Square. The driver was travelling at great speed and it was obvious that he wouldn't make the bend into Lowndes Square – he didn't!

The car hit the kerb with a bang and then hit the railings and as it did so it hit a large tree. It came to rest standing on its rear end, facing up the tree. We ran over and opened the door and saw the agony on the face of a young boy in the driver's seat. When we looked down we saw both his feet were hanging on only by a small piece of skin. I tried to console him as best I could by trying to stop the bleeding until the ambulance came and took him to hospital.

After spending a long time in hospital to recover from this terrible accident, the driver appeared at the Magistrates Court charged with numerous driving offences, including stealing the vehicle and causing criminal damage. The atmosphere in court was tense and when the facts were given you could hear a pin drop. The young lad sat in a wheel-chair swathed in bandages — everyone knew that he had no feet. The Magistrate asked the boy's parents to come forward but there was no reply. The boy was alone. It gave the crowd something to think about. The Magistrate broke the silence and in a voice full of emotion he said, 'You've learned a lesson in a terrible way and you will suffer the consequences of your actions for the rest of your life in a manner which I hope none of us will ever have to endure. Let this be your only punishment.' The Magistrate then wished him good luck as he returned to his rehabilitation centre.

We felt the urge to cheer the decision which I thought was the right one, but how does someone cope with life after losing both feet and being all alone in the world?

One night duty I was on patrol in Knightsbridge when I came across a mishap with two vehicles – one had shunted into the rear of the other. I asked the first driver what had happened and if anyone was injured. I then asked the second driver the same questions but when I saw who he was I couldn't keep a straight face because he was giving us his act from his television show from the previous night. It was Peter Cook. I said to him, 'I'm sorry Peter but every time I see you, I can't help but laugh.' He then cracked a joke about the Queen's corgis and he said to me, 'You see Officer, that's what I'm here for to, make people laugh. The world needs more laughter, that's why I ran into this car.' The small crowd which had by now gathered roared with laughter. I then said to both drivers, 'I'm sorry but I've got a job to do, just exchange names and addresses and I'll be on my way.' I left Peter Cook still entertaining the public at the scene. It was nice to see such good humour turning this 'crisis' around; we could do with more of it.

I was turning my own crisis into as much pleasure as I could as I lay in my hospital bed. It was fifteen days since I had had my first operation. I'd just let out a yell of pain as a big nurse came to turn me over. I was still unable to move on my own and had to be turned like an oven chicken to get the other side done. It was nine months since I'd sat up and I couldn't even hold my head up for long, but I could still do certain exercises and was still enjoying the occasional bed bath.

When I'd been there for nearly twenty days a Mrs Israel came to see me. She was to be my physiotherapist for the next two months or so. She said to me, 'We will now sit you up' – and she did just that! My head was spinning as if I'd been on a bender for six months. The pain was awful because my back was now infected and puss was coming out of the wound.

In fact, the whole hospital, including the operating theatre, was closed, because everywhere was infected with something or other. People were becoming very ill. I was told that I hadn't infected the other patients, it was the hospital that was infecting everyone else. Each ward was vacated in turn as the disinfecting machine was taken round. The whole hospital was scrubbed and washed. I'd never seen so many walking wounded in my life. It was like a battlefield. When I saw a young child in a worse condition than me, it made me more positive and I thought, 'I *will* walk again.'

Time went by and Mrs Israel got me sitting up in bed. Then she stood me on a box at the side of the bed. A few days later I took my first step. The following day I took the next step until after twenty-one days I managed to walk to the table for my first meal out of bed. It was the most beautiful meal I had ever eaten. I'll always remember what I had – it was chicken curry and rice and I had a whole breast of chicken.

My back was in such a mess that they couldn't take my stitches out so they stayed put, as I did. Lying comfortably in my bed and thinking of my achievement of walking, I started looking back again on my good old days as a police officer.

I remember the biggest accident I ever had to deal with. It was a very dark, cold and rainy evening. I arrived to find a double-decker bus was balanced precariously over a large hole that Council workmen had dug in the road outside a public house. A large compressor was on its side and petrol from its tank was pouring into the pub cellar. In the hole in the road, with the bus teetering above it, was a mini with two occupants trapped inside and the hole was rapidly filling with water. It was like a Training School exercise, but his was real life!

Apparently the bus had skidded across the road when it braked to avoid a car pulling away from the kerb-side. It hit the mini coming in the opposite direction. The bus knocked the car into the hole, smashing the guard-rails and knocking the compressor over. In the crash, fifty gallons of petrol had poured into the pub cellar from the compressor's petrol tank.

I called for back-up – ambulance, fire brigade and a London Transport crane – and jumped into the hole. The passengers in the car were safe for the time being but no matter how much I tried, I could not get them out, so they calmly sat there and waited to be rescued. I got some people to sit on the bus as a counter-balance to prevent it falling any further into the hole.

The ambulance arrived first so I got the injured people in the bus off to hospital. When the fire brigade came they pumped the hole dry and washed the petrol out of the pub cellar.

We put timbers across the hole to hold the bus, until the crane could lift it clear. The crane was then driven nearer the hole and I jumped in and put the harness around the mini. I had been an engineer so I knew what needed to be done. The mini was slowly lifted clear of the hole and set down on the road and the occupants were released and taken to hospital where they were treated for shock and given a general check over.

A tow truck was sent from a garage to remove all the vehicles. The compressor was returned to its upright position and made safe, the Council placed fresh guards round the hole and new lamps were lit and put in place. The pub was made safe and the bus was removed to the garage. One pedestrian, twelve bus passengers and two car passengers were taken to hospital. God I was tired out! And wet through from the continuous drizzle. By this time, I had worked four hours over my eight-hour shift, and I was ravenous.

I went to the hospital and saw all the injured, recorded their names and addresses, interviewed the doctors, and contacted the bus depot regarding damage to the bus. It was now two-thirty in the morning and I had been working since 7am, so I had been on duty for over 19 hours.

I returned to the nick and the new Sergeant who was on duty told me off for not reporting in! You can imagine what a mouthful he got from me. It took me two hours to write my reports and when had I finished I took it to the Sergeant who checked them. He said, 'This is rubbish.' and tore them in half and threw them out of the window into the basement. He then said, 'Go and get them and rewrite them.' Well that put the tin hat on it. I was going to grab him and smack him one but instead I said to him, as Sam said to the officer when he knocked his musket off his shoulder, 'Thou knocked it down and thou picks it up or it stays where it is on the floor.' He repeated again, 'Go and pick the report up, rewrite it and then bring it to me.' I was tired and in great need of a shower, so I said, 'I'm tired, I've been on duty 20 hours and I'm going home, and if you don't want to pick yourself up out of the basement, I suggest you remove your body from my path and let me pass.' The Duty Inspector was present and he told me to go home. Afterwards I learnt he had ordered the Sergeant pick up the report and remain on duty and rewrite it. The Sergeant was then posted off the division and was never to be seen again. I slept peacefully that night. By the way, no petrol or water got into the beer.

I was now regarded as the rebel of Royal 'A' Division, but all the senior officers agreed with my action, I think.

I remember another stupid accident that I was called to and I still laugh about it today. When I got to the venue, I saw a man in his pyjamas standing by a car that had crashed into a tree in his front drive. I wondered whether he had been sleepwalking, or if he had driven into the

house and out through the bedroom window. However, neither explanation was right. When another man appeared, I asked him what had
happened. He said, 'I drove into my drive and hit the tree, then I knew it
wasn't my drive because I haven't got a tree.' The pyjama-clad man then
added, 'I was in bed at the time and he is trespassing and I want compensation for the loss of my tree.' I asked if anyone had been injured but no
one had, so I said to the two men, 'Then you will have to take action
yourselves. Goodnight.'

>◦◦<

I'd like to tell you about an accident that occurred a good many years
later. It was both tragic and amusing – but the underdog had his day.

My son had booked a church hall for his wedding on a Saturday in
August. On the day before the wedding it was my task to run down to the
hall with barrels of beer, cases of wine, sherry, port, spirits, cutlery, as
well as plates and drinking glasses. So I called at the various stores to
pick up these items in my Volvo 740 estate. My son was the passenger
and we set off for the hall. The load was strapped into place and we went
through Golders Green towards West Hampstead. After a while it began
to rain so I took my time going down the hill passing by Hampstead
Heath. I could see there were vehicles parked on both sides of the road so
I took extra care. As I approached the bottom of the hill, I saw a large van
double-parked on the opposite side of the road. My side was clear so I
proceeded to go though. However, I stepped on my brakes and stopped
quickly when a stupid driver pulled out from behind the large van at
speed and hit the front of my Volvo.

The car that hit mine was a police panda car. The driver looked about
22 years old and the passenger was the Commander of the district, who
was late for a meeting, hence the rate of knots at which the car was being
driven. I jumped out of my car and saw the other car's front wheels were
touching its back wheels – the car had bent in two! I looked inside the
police vehicle and saw the Commander was in a terrible state. His head
was split open across the forehead and he was covered in blood. The
driver was also cut and bruised. I used his radio to call for assistance and
for an ambulance. As I did so I noticed the driver of the large white van
start to drive away. I shouted to him, 'I'm a police officer, don't you dare
move that van.' He stayed put and the police arrived and closed off the

street. The ambulance arrived next and took away the injured policemen.

The reporting officer informed me that the police constable driver was in fact an Assistant Commissioner's son. It was still pouring with rain as it always does when something like this happens and as the officer made out his report the rain poured off his helmet and onto his report book.

The Garage Sergeant, an independent officer, took measurements at the scene of the accident and put together a full report. He told me that in his opinion the accident did not appear to be my fault. As I waited at the scene, I took the names of a couple of witnesses to the accident, together with my son's evidence. I thought that I was on solid ground, but that is where I was wrong.

The police car was lifted onto the back of a lorry and taken away. I was told I could leave so I drove off with only slight damage to my car. The weight of my Volvo and its big bumper bars had saved us. Our load was also undamaged, so off we went.

Two weeks later I was told to report to Hampstead Police Station where the Chief Superintendent interviewed me. His first words were, 'You have been reported for dangerous, careless and reckless driving.' He then cautioned me and asked me if I wished to make a statement. I told him to get lost because the allegation was a complete load of rubbish. He then said, 'You don't even have a witness to support your version of what happened at the accident,' I replied, 'That's funny, my son was with me and I have two other private witnesses from the scene.' This got under his skin and he became annoyed and shouted, 'Your son is too young to be a witness.' I said, 'But he got married the day after the accident and he is 24 years old.' He then asked for the details of my son and I said, 'If you couldn't take them at the scene, then I'm not going to give them to you now.'

That really got him going. He opened his desk drawer and flung a brand new Personal Injury Accident Book at me and said, 'Look for yourself, no witnesses, so you're in the wrong, you haven't got a leg to stand on.' I laughed, which disturbed him even more, and I told him, 'I've got you now for aiding and abetting perjury and I will be reporting you.' He asked me what I meant, so I told him that it is an offence to alter a report book. He had obviously done this because the original report book would have been wet through due to the rain. I repeated that it was perjury, as information had been transferred from one book to another and that during the course of the transfer of notes some pertinent pieces of information had been omitted. He shouted, *'Get out!'* So off I went.

I suppose they must have got together because I was later asked to return to the Chief Superintendent's office accompanied by my son. We both made statements. I was allowed to read my son's statement and I knew I couldn't have done it any better because his statement was clear, precise, truthful and accurate.

We then returned to the Chief Super's office where he asked me to drop the allegation of perjury. (He must have taken some legal advice). His temper rose again when I refused and he threw the accident book at me. I told him there were mistakes that the officer had made. He asked me to show him where. I was only bluffing, but pretended to thumb through the pages. In the box for the witness statement was my son's name and his new address and a supposed 'statement' by him. I showed it to him and said, 'You've made things worse now, you have added my son's name and address. But you see, on this day in August when the accident occurred and even up to the beginning of this week, my son had no idea he would be living there. My barrister would pick this up straightaway and prove you are not telling the truth.' By now very irate, the Super yelled *'Get out!'*

There must have been a high level talk with the Yard's legal team, and I know they spoke to the Garage Sergeant who had reported the accident, because the following week I received a letter from the Legal Department of Scotland Yard. The gist of it was that the charges against me had been dropped and a cheque for £1,300 was enclosed for damages.

Thinking more about this incident, I wonder what would have happened if I had been an ordinary member of the public with no knowledge of the law. It worries me to think about it. The Chief Superintendent had bent over backwards to save the young driver at the expense of a fellow officer – myself – in order to pacify the higher authorities. But right triumphed over wrong in the end.

I had known this sort of thing to happen before when a police officer summonsed about fifteen cars in a Belgravia mews for parking offences. They all pleaded 'Guilty' at court and were fined. However, it wasn't an offence to park cars in the Mews in those days because they were on private property and a driver could not be fined for parking on private property. I learned this later because I was that Police Officer!

I only heard about the following story so I cannot vouch for its accuracy.

A woman had an accident in her car in the south of France one night. She reported the accident to police and gave them the registration number of the other vehicle. The number was flashed to Interpol who sent it to Scotland Yard because it was the number of one of the Met's 'Q' cars. The driver was to be reported for failing to stop after an accident.

To have been in France as had been suggested would have meant that the car would have had to have been driven about 1,500 miles, crossed the channel and back, been repaired and re-sprayed, in time for the crew to be back in the UK in time for breakfast. Nonetheless, the crew was duly sent for and they were all required to make statements.

It transpired that they had commenced duty at 6pm and finished at 6am and at no time did they go the South of France. Furthermore they had all been seen during the night at the Police Station!

It's strange, but members of the public are always the first to be believed in these situations. How daft!

My interview for the CID came and I was thrilled when I was selected to be a temporary detective. After being accepted I was told to report to Detective Chief Superintendent Fred Lambert at Chelsea Police Station on 'B' Division to begin my CID service. I had known Fred when he served at Gerald Road; he recognised me and wished me good luck.

Chapter Thirteen

CHELSEA CID

All new CID officers have to undergo an introductory course on crime, CID procedures and investigation. During this course my brain worked overtime; it was kicked into shape and I wondered afterwards how I had managed previously.

As an example, we were each given a copy of a photograph taken at the scene of a serious crime and told to study it and identify all the clues. As we sat in silence, a man rushed into the room and shouted, 'Who believes that I'm barmy?' He then ran out again. We continued to study the photograph until the end of the allotted time when the photographs were collected and we sat with pencil and paper at the ready.

We had been tricked because the first thing the Instructor asked us was: 'Describe the man who ran into the room a minute ago.' After we attempted to do so the instructor told us to write down all the clues we had found in the photograph. I coped, but only just. My mind never wandered from then on and I was prepared for any repetition of this sort of occurrence.

Our classroom was adjacent to one being used by Detective Chief Superintendent Tommy Butler who was investigating a murder case. I had been doing some enquiries on behalf of the Nottinghamshire Police and I was awaiting a telephone call. In error, my caller had been given Tommy Butler's number. Butler walked into our room and told me to take a call on his telephone. When I'd done so, he took me to one side and gave me a piece of his mind. I told him it was not my fault that someone had been given the wrong number. He seemed to accept my explanation but he was not amused when I said, 'We are both on the same side, aren't we?' At the end of the course I had to sit another examination, which I was thrilled to pass, and then I returned to Chelsea Police Station.

I was sent to Hyde Park to take part in an investigation into a murder. A young boy had thrown a brick from the Serpentine Bridge over the lake and a passing rower had been struck on the back of the head. He died later in hospital. We had to interview anyone who had been in the Park at the time of the incident and eventually the culprit was traced and taken Juvenile Court – where he got his knuckles wrapped!

A call was received from a refuse collector at the local rubbish tip who had emptied a dustbin and had seen an arm disappearing into the crusher. They had taken the load to the collection centre. I went to the centre, which was in Fulham. Armed with cigars, rubber gloves and protective wear, I cleared a square of concrete, where the load had been tipped out and began a painstaking search. I scraped every piece of garbage to one side, not only looking for a body but for any evidence relating to the offence – the offence being the concealment of a death.

I soon came across the body of a baby boy. I placed him gently in a box we had set side for the purpose, but our job did not end there. It was necessary for the remainder of the load to be systematically searched. The only thing we were sure of was that the bin bag, which had contained the body, had come from an address in Redcliffe Road, in Fulham.

The Coroner carried out an examination of the body and concluded that the baby had been born dead and not murdered. After extensive enquiries a report was submitted to this effect. We would only open the case if any further evidence came to light, but anyone, even a passing motorist, could have dumped the little baby in the bin.

The next job I was given was to go to an underground burial chamber which prisoners from Wormwood Scrubs had been sent to clean up. In this underground chamber the coffins were placed in the wall, which could be easily seen by the viewer through a locked grille. The chamber had seats by the pillars that held up the roof. It was in a disgusting state. The grilles were rotting away with age, as were the coffins. Some trustees from a group of prisoners were sent to clear up the mess until the job was complete. However, someone hadn't thought ahead because when the prisoners were released, the chamber was ransacked. An observation had to be put in place.

First Class Detective Sergeant Alan George worked out a rota for us to go down into this terrible place at night to carry out an observation. He explained that there had been burials there since the Battle of Trafalgar; bodies were buried with all their regalia, swords, medals and the like, which as you can imagine were quite valuable. It was arranged for two officers to be present at any one time.

When it came my turn to watch the prisoners, the room was wet and dank and the wind whistled down the entrance, seemingly with nowhere to go except up my trouser leg, and it was freezing cold. The scene was worse than anything a Frankenstein film could throw at us. We could see where the coffins had been broken and skulls were actually showing. It was distinctly frightening. I also noticed that by one of the pillars water was pouring in but I couldn't find out where it was going.

Anyway, two officers went down one particular night and apparently one of them laid some cardboard down by one of the pillars. He sat down and soon dropped off to sleep. The other officer put his hand into the freezing water that was running down one of the pillars and held it there for as long as he could. He then ran his icy hand over his sleeping mate's face who promptly woke up with a blood-curdling scream and ran for the entrance as though his life depended upon it. He didn't stop running until he got back to the nick. Practically in tears, he told everyone about the ghostly figure that had carried out the dastardly deed. The other officer was not going to stay by himself in that ghastly place so he was close on his colleague's heels. The observation was called off after this because no one would go there again.

The frightened officer would love to know who the ghost was that night, but that 'ghost' has never admitted his terrible deed. I could not stop laughing about the incident and I still chuckle about it now.

On my first night duty as a new CID officer I was with Detective Sergeant Thompson-Smith, a Scotsman of good order. He was a fine copper and a good friend. We managed to acquire information that drugs could be obtained at a certain address in Chelsea, so we went there posing as customers.

We were welcomed into the premises, which was full of television, radio, film and theatre artists. Unfortunately, a great many of them had been partaking of the drugs that were on offer. Other officers were waiting in surrounding streets and at a given signal arrests were made. As more customers arrived, they were duly arrested and processed as the others had been. By the time we arrived at the nick, newspaper reporters were everywhere. I was surrounded and jostled for a top story, even for days after.

It was three days after this event before we could go home for a scrub and a change of clothes. We had made twenty-seven arrests for crime, and had collected thousands of pounds worth of drugs. We were told to keep the names of the people arrested completely confidential. Most of those artists were very famous then, and some still are today.

One of my first arrests after a full investigation of my own was that of Martin Conan-Doyle, the grandson of the famous author, for fraud. He had been calling at various shops where he had been 'flying kites' (a slang term for buying goods by cheque, knowing there are no funds to honour it.) I arrested him and took him to Court. He took £35 to court to pay off the creditors and he told the Magistrate that he would pay them what he owed, so he was given a Conditional Discharge.

As we were leaving the Court he asked a few of us to go for a drink with him. He took them to the local pub and very generously bought them all drinks until he found out he was broke, made a quick getaway and the officers were landed with the bill.

Life's like that!

I heard of a case that day where police had stopped a young lad who was found to be carrying drugs. He later appeared at court. The police officer went into the witness box to ask for a remand until the drug could be analysed. The Magistrate asked the police officer what he thought the drug was and he replied 'cannabis'. The Magistrate then asked the defendant what he thought the drug was and the defendant also said 'cannabis'. The drug was passed up to the Magistrate who smelled the substance, looked at it and even tasted it (he must have seen this done on the telly), and then said, 'If we all agree it is cannabis, we can carry on with the case.'

The defendant was asked, 'How do you plead?' The reply was, 'Not guilty,' so the officer began to give his evidence, which was as follows. 'I stopped the defendant in Piccadilly, and when he was searched we found in his underpants, between his legs, this piece of cannabis resin.' Well, upon hearing this, the Magistrate turned a little green and immediately adjourned the case. After he had speedily disappeared from the courtroom, the Court was in uproar. I am sure the next time he had a similar case, he took a very different line of questioning.

In those early days we did quite a lot of patrolling within our designated patch. On one occasion as we were patrolling around Earls Court, a likely place for villains at the time, I saw a sports car being driven the wrong way down a one-way street.

Forgetting I was no longer a uniformed officer, I jumped out of the patrol car and stopped the driver. I told him that I was a police officer and that he was going the wrong way down a one-way street. To my amazement the driver was none other than Stirling Moss. (He was definitely not a villain). It's a good job it was him or I would probably not be writing this now. He pointed out that it had not been a one-way street the day before. When I checked it out, I found that he was right!

I was sitting at my desk when a letter was thrown into my in-tray. I quickly read the contents and saw it was from a lady in the World's End area who stated that her next-door neighbour was stealing petrol. Unfortunately, I couldn't deal with it straight away and it was two days before I had an opportunity to check out her story. I obtained a search warrant and went to the address armed with the warrant.

The owner of the flat answered the door. He was a trainee taxi driver. I showed him the warrant and entered the premises. It was a small studio flat and comprised of a sitting room/bedroom and a kitchen. In the one room there was a table, chairs and a bed. Two small children were in the bed. I searched the room but did not find any petrol. The man was adamant that he had no petrol, but he went a little pale when we went outside and I found eight gallons of the stuff.

We re-entered the flat where his wife took some money from the mantelpiece, which she said they had saved for a holiday. She said, 'I've £13 here, take it and please don't take us to Court.' I told her that it was an offence to bribe a police officer and advised her to put the money away.

The man told us that his brother who owned a garage had given him the petrol. I knew that his brother would automatically corroborate his story and that we would be wasting our time, so I decided to give him the benefit of the doubt. He could possibly have been guilty of some crime so I said, 'I'm leaving now, but if there is any petrol still here when I return, I'll nick you'.

I went back to the address later but there was no sign of any petrol. I said to the man's wife, 'Never, ever try to bribe a police officer or you will be in worse trouble. If there is one thing I can't stand it is a bent copper.' I then told the husband that I would be watching his every move.

As it happened, they went on a holiday with their money and they also moved to a new house. The husband was very successful in his taxi business and, hopefully, he appreciated that crime doesn't pay. Having been given a second chance, he was able to make good.

A woman alleged that a demolition workman and his son had knocked on her door and asked if she had any antiques or the like for sale. They stayed for a chat, but when they had gone so too had her antique mantelpiece clock.

I must mention at this point that the whole of the Worlds End was being demolished and the workmen knew there were rich pickings to be had. So they went from house to house offering to buy anything worth a bob or two. I found out later that they had quite a haul, but I couldn't prove it.

Eventually they were arrested and elected for trial by jury. I knew we would have difficulty proving the case, but then I had a stroke of luck. The case had started when I received information that the stolen clock was in a local antique shop. The owner of the shop had the name and address of the seller – it was the person we had in court. On the instruction of Counsel, I brought the shop owner and the clock to court. When the prisoner saw the shop owner and the clock he collapsed. So did his case!

He was fined and ordered to pay costs exceeding the value of the property he had obtained from his victims. Justice was done, and seen to be done.

———○———

Some days nothing happened but on this particular day a bundle of things happened. I was in the Earl's Court area when a young woman drove past in a mini-car at great speed. When the car reached the end of the road it hit the kerb, bounced into the air and fell straight down onto a spiked fence. There was a brief pause before it slipped further down the spikes, which pierced the car and went straight through the driver's body. We raced up to the car and immediately saw that the driver was dead.

There was unfortunately nothing we could do. It certainly knocked the stuffing out of us for the rest of that day.

That same evening, we were called to a lesbians' club in Chelsea, just off the Kings Road. I'd been to other punch-ups and fights between violent people, but nothing I had experienced thus far compared with this. Dozens of women were fighting each other, hair was being pulled out; skin was being ripped off, and the violence was the worst I'd ever seen. Then a false leg came flying across our path. (So someone was obviously legless!) We waited for uniform back-up before daring to interfere and we eventually managed to gain control of the situation. When things returned to normal, we found that the injuries ranged from cuts and bruises, to broken arms, broken wrists and even broken noses.

When women fight it is best to stand back and not interfere. I speak from experience. Once when I was in uniform I came across a husband and wife fighting in the street. I parted them and pointed out the errors of their ways but as I turned my back on the wife to speak to her husband she picked up a piece of wood and before I could stop her she struck me on top of my head. She then carried on fighting with her husband and, would you believe it, when they stopped they went home arm in arm! *Til death them do part.*

During the Sixties, drugs were all the rage in Chelsea, especially in the King's Road. In fact, in those days, young people challenged all the rules, but drugs were our main concern. I topped sixty arrests for drug offences in my first year with the CID. There were twenty other officers who had roughly the same number of arrests, so you can imagine the mountain we had to climb. Burglary was our second biggest problem, which was also a major problem for all the Stations on our Division.

We had our share of murders, attempted murders, assaults, rapes, and lots of thefts. There was also a mixture of minor crime to deal with but I loved doing the job and relished my workload. I even became an accomplished typist and after a day's work I would spend half the night typing out my reports.

I also spent a lot of time making court appearances, sometimes five times a week. On some days, I had to appear in two different courts in the same day. Which brings me to my next story.

One morning I was summoned to Marlborough Street Court and travelled there on the underground from South Kensington. As I stood on the platform waiting for a train a pigeon appeared and landed beside me. As soon as the train doors opened the pigeon hopped on board. It stood in the doorway and when the train stopped at the next station it hopped off and flew away. This happened four mornings in a row.

I thought of arresting it for travelling without a ticket, but the Guvnor would only have given me the bird. Then I thought, is it a police spy, a rubber heeler watching us? ('Rubber heelers' was the name given to police officers who were employed to keep surveillance on other police officers who were suspected of having committed offences.) Perhaps this was their new secret weapon.

So I forgot about my pigeon until one day in the Earls Court area I saw a man acting suspiciously. I watched him until I couldn't stand it anymore and then went up to him, announced who I was, and asked him what he was doing, 'Just watch that wall,' he said. I thought I must be as barmy as him as I stared at the brick wall. All of a sudden, out of a hole came some bubbles, which floated away. Then it happened again, and again.

We both became addicted to watching these bloody bubbles but we couldn't find out how or why they were coming from a small hole in a brick wall.

The man turned to me and said, 'Oh by the way, my name is Andrew Ray, Ted Ray's son. I work for the BBC and I'm doing a programme on television concerning strange inexplicable incidents'. (His father was a big star at the time.) As we talked, I told him about my rubber heeler – the criminal pigeon that failed every day to pay its fare.

Despite our investigations the pigeon never appeared again. Either some other officer had arrested it or it had wanted a change of scenery and caught the pigeon post express. God help me, I am going barmy!

Night duty came around again and I was working with Detective Sergeant Jim Hanscombe who was dealing with an enquiry on behalf of Notting Hill Police Station when a call came in from a member of the public who had heard a woman screaming. Similar calls also came in from other members of the public in the street. Jim told me to go and find out what was happening. I arrived at the scene with another officer and heard the screams coming from the second floor of a house. I tried but couldn't get in (front doors in Notting Hill are like castle doors and need to be) so I broke a window on the ground floor, crept inside, opened the door and let my partner in.

We soon discovered that we had just broken into a brothel (and not paid our dues). We rushed up to the room where the screaming had come from, opened the door and saw a disgusting sight. A young girl was lying on the bed underneath a man. They were both naked. The man was built like a mountain and folds of his flesh fell over the girl and partly over the bed. He was huge. The girl shouted, 'Get him off, get him off.' I went up to him and saw that he was dead! He'd had a heart attack and died, trapping the girl beneath him. She couldn't budge him. We were joined by another police officer and it took all three of us to roll the man over and off the girl. I left the uniformed police constable to deal with reporting the matter.

It is always when you are enjoying yourself that someone or something spoils it for you, but what a way to go.

On the same night duty with Jim Hanscombe, we were taking a break. I had just picked up a glass of Coca-Cola and a small snack of fried eggs, bacon, mushrooms and baked beans at the British Airways Canteen in Cromwell Road. I had just sat down when an urgent call came through from Information Room at Scotland Yard for us to telephone them from a call box. You can imagine our reaction at having to leave our delicious supper. Instructions like these often indicate the nature of the incident. Usually they relate to incidents involving VIPs, and call boxes are used so as to prevent other people, i.e. the press, listening in.

We were told that a man had been detained after breaking into Princess Margaret's apartments at Kensington Palace. Jim and I were told to make our way there. When we arrived we immediately arrested the man and took him to the nick. It was discovered that a letter had been left at the Palace but it had not been opened, so Detective Chief Superintendent Fred Lambert was sent for and he questioned the arrested man. As was thought, our prisoner had left the letter. He claimed to be a friend of Princess Margaret and he said that he had been trying to talk to her for sometime, but she always refused to talk to him. The letter was returned to the Palace but we were never told what its contents were. The following day, the press was present in force at the court. Where they had got their information from I'll never know. There must be a mole in every nick. Fred Lambert went into the witness box and gave evidence, but all the press wanted to know was why he had been called to deal with a minor case such as this. They started digging, but they couldn't find out – and neither could we lowly police officers. There was a massive cover up somewhere and we could only guess why. Was it possible that the man was a closer friend of the Princess than we originally thought? We will never know.

A call came my way one night to go to a house in the Little Boltons. When I arrived a woman and her daughter met me. The woman explained that they had rented one of their furnished houses to a man who had provided good references. However, on visiting the property, she found that the house was completely empty so she rang the police. I took a description and the name of the man and made some checks at the Yard. I soon found the information I needed and together with another officer I went off to the German Beer Keller in Earls Court Road. We recognised the man and arrested him.

We learned from him where most of the furniture was, so we made our way to a block of flats in the Earls Court area. I knocked on the door and a man answered. When he was informed who we were and what we had come for he was very upset, to put it mildly. However, he was not so upset as his wife when we tipped her out of the bed we had come to repossess. They must have slept on the floor for the rest of the night. It was the same procedure at each address until we had returned the furniture to the original house.

The furniture was photographed, the man was charged and he received his just deserts. But there were a lot of unhappy people who had unknowingly paid good money for stolen property.

I was having a great time in the CID and one night I was told to go with another officer to a well-known nightclub to keep observation. The nightclub was called 'Blaizes', an apt name in the circumstances because its sister club had been blown up and destroyed during the gangland wars of the time.

During the time we were there we were given drinks and a meal each evening. However, we were a little frightened because a bomb could have come winging our way at any time and no one in the Club would have had much chance of escaping. The place was absolutely packed every evening, so it was always a good idea to keep an exit clear.

On the third night, the club closed at 2.30am and I was walking home when I saw two men carrying iron bars and trying to break into cars. I watched them for a minute or two and then walked up behind them and told them who I was. Well I nearly did, because I made them both jump. The first man in his fright whacked me across the face with a tyre-lever and cut my forehead and split my eye open. The two men ran off and I staggered to Gerald Road Police Station, which was nearby.

I was sent to St George's Hospital where I was duly stitched and patched up by the medical staff and kept in for the night before being discharged the following morning. As I came out of the hospital at Hyde

Park Corner, I saw a news-stand with a large banner headline reading 'DETECTIVE ATTACKED WITH A SPANNER!' I thought that it might be a good idea to buy a paper and that I might even know who the detective was. I read the article and when I saw the name 'Detective Constable Beard' I thought to myself, you bloody idiot. It was indeed about me. Some detective! Someone had moved quickly to get this in the newspaper. I later found out that the Sergeant had authorised the observation at the Club without authority and now he was in trouble. I felt sorry for the mess he was in.

I was having a difficult time at home because my wife was very ill. She had to have two operations on her legs and she also needed a hysterectomy, so it was a tough period, and I did my best to keep the house running with at least some semblance of normality. Fred Lambert sent for me when he heard what was going on and gave me an inside job. He told me to come in when I liked and leave when I needed to. If I needed to take any time off, then it was okay by him. I had my two lads to look after, getting them to school as well as doing the shopping, the housework and the cooking.

   This went on for about six weeks. My poor wife had one hundred and eleven sutures in her legs and she was very weak. We managed to get her back home, but she had to be lifted in and out of the bath and because of this and so many other tasks I spent more and more time at home.

   I knew that police life had to go on but I noticed jealousy creeping in when a senior officer ordered me to go with him to Great Yarmouth where we were to investigate a serious crime. Well you can imagine my lack of enthusiasm, but his response was, 'Either go to Great Yarmouth or resign, what's it to be?' I asked for time to arrange for my family to be looked after and then went with him to Great Yarmouth. We did the job where six villains were arrested for a well-publicised robbery at the time. Then it was back to my family who were safe and well.

   But the next time I went to the nick I slapped my resignation on my Guvnor's desk and in the section entitled 'Reasons for resignation', I set out the whole story.

   Fred Lambert, who had been very sympathetic, sent for me. He granted me compassionate leave and after he accepted my resignation –

but only from the CID – he endorsed it by adding to his report, *'As soon as time permits and this officer and his family are completely recovered, I strongly recommend he comes back into the CID.'*

Three months later I was back in the CID, but instead of returning to Chelsea I was posted to Canon Row Police Station, where I was mainly assigned to Royalty Protection duties. The Detective Sergeant there was Roger Matthews, whom I had known for a long time. By the end of his distinguished career he reached the rank of Chief Superintendent. He had the job of re-opening the enquiry on James Hanratty who, you may recall, was wrongly hanged for the murder and attempted murder of a couple in a car on the A6. Roger proved that Hanratty was innocent of the crime.

Between my Royalty Protection duty, I had a case in which I arrested a man who had committed a lot of thefts in the West End and in Haymarket. He had been detained in one store where he had carried out one theft too many. I went into the manager's office and saw a scruffily dressed individual slumped in a drunken stupor at a table where numerous bottles of whisky were laid out in front of him. The bottles had been found in concealed pockets of his large overcoat after a search had been carried out. I took him to Cannon Row and decided to check out his background. I found out that he was Irish and he was wanted in Dublin for a robbery that had been carried out at an off-licence.

When he sobered up he admitted the robbery at the off-licence, so I decided to contact the Guarda in Dublin and ask for someone to come to London and bring the warrant for the prisoner's extradition to Ireland. I picked up the telephone, dialled the number, and heard a click at the other end as someone picked up the telephone. A voice said, 'Guarda'. I said, 'Metropolitan Police.' That's all I got to say as he stopped me short and said, 'No, this is The Guarda, the Metropolitan Police is in London' and with that he put the telephone down. I thought to myself, 'Now that's Irish for you.' (Don't get me wrong, I love the Irish, my daughter-in-law is Irish and her parents are wonderful people.)

I rang again and asked for the CID; this time the telephone call went according to plan and I was assured that an officer would be sent to pick up my alcoholic prisoner. A couple of days later the officer duly arrived, picked up the prisoner and escorted him back to the Emerald Isle, where he had to be satisfied with Irish whiskey – or maybe plain water for a while.

One hot summer's day, a member of the public called me and asked me to meet him in St James' Park to investigate a number of alleged indecent offences. Evidently a man, who was well known to the caller, had carried out the offences and the informant was able to point him out to me.

I decided to keep my observation confined to the Park. After a couple of hours the alleged offender arrived and I saw him approach some young boys. I was horrified to see him put his hand down the trousers of one of them. I went up to him and showed him my warrant card, told him what I'd seen, arrested him there and then and escorted him back to Cannon Row.

I took possession of his front door keys and, accompanied by another officer, I went to his house which was nearby, to carry out a search. It didn't take us long to find pornographic books mainly on homosexuality with young boys. We also found photographs of young boys in embarrassing situations. We confiscated his address book and took it back to the Police Station for a thorough check. After a painstaking trawl through all the addresses we were able to locate a number of young boys who lived locally. We called the lads and their parents into the Police Station to question them.

I asked one boy who had appeared in quite a few of the photographs to provide a statement to enable us to charge the prisoner, but to our astonishment, he refused. He told us, ' I won't say anything against him because I love him.' It transpired that the man ran a newspaper shop and over a period of five years he had committed buggery with all of his paperboys. In fact some of the young boys in the photographs were now adults.

However, just when it seemed that we were getting no further with our investigation we came up trumps when we interviewed a nineteen-year old lad who had been deeply traumatised by the paedophile and was willing to stand up in court and testify against him. So the man was charged, placed in a cell and – sometime later – convicted.

Night duty soon came around at Cannon Row and one particular night there was an armed robbery at a block of government offices. The night cleaners were still on the premises when the robbery occurred. We drew our firearms and attended the scene. The cleaners were clearly shaken by what had occurred so near to where they had been working but when they calmed down we were able to interview them. The manager arrived and found that the only cash that had been taken was the cleaners' wages, which amounted to about a couple of thousand pounds.

The cleaners' statements included some very useful information. One of the cleaners knew the gang and she was able to tell us that they were from Brixton. After some in-depth questioning it emerged that another of the cleaners was in collusion with the gang of robbers. She was taken to the Station where we were able to very quickly establish her involvement in the robbery. She blabbed all the information (and more besides) that we required about this and other robberies committed by the gang. She was an ideal witness!

We went to Brixton Police Station where we saw the officer who had been waiting for us. We all went to the Collator's office to get whatever information there was on the gang and then went to 'spin their drums' (search their houses). We banged on the first door and it was opened almost immediately. With guns at the ready we moved inside. I made my way upstairs and cautiously opened the door of one of the bedrooms. I entered the room slowly and began searching it. As I was looking under the bed, the wardrobe doors suddenly burst open and out jumped one of the villains. He made me jump so high that I almost rebounded off the ceiling and my little old 'ticker' was pounding under the rib cage at an exceptionally fast rate of knots. My training kicked in and I grabbed him, banged his head against the wall and handcuffed him before he had a chance to retaliate. (Later I reflected on what I had done especially when I learnt that he had a gun, and I thought to myself what an idiot I had been for taking such a risk. But at the time you simply swing into autopilot). The villain began laughing hysterically as we headed along the landing towards the top of the stairs and then, without hesitating, he lurched forward out of my reach in an attempt to throw himself down the stairs. (I had a vision of future newspaper headlines: *'Robbery case dropped due to police brutality.'*)

Working purely on instinct I grabbed him and with all my strength (he was a very big guy) hung on to him and yelled for immediate assistance from my colleagues. The officers ran to my aid and I was extremely pleased to be able to say to the assailant, 'No compensation for you this time, my friend. You're heading for prison, make no mistake about that!'

Later at the Magistrate's Court, reports were submitted which said that the suspect had the mental age of a ten-year-old and that he was unfit to plead. You'll not be surprised to hear that the so-called experts' reports swung the case around and the suspect was able to walk away happily from the crime. The problem was that although he had been found unfit to be tried in a court of law he was not unfit to commit further crimes – this he did extensively.

Unfortunately, it was now my turn to be ill. I was off work for some time as I had been found to have a tumour. Once the tumour had been diagnosed I was immediately admitted to hospital to have an operation to remove it. After it was removed I was sent to the police nursing home in Hove for three weeks.

The Matron at the nursing home was a stickler for rules and regulations and she was certainly from the old school of nursing. We convalescing officers had other ideas. We were allowed to go out as part of our recovery, but we had strict instructions to be back by 10pm or we would be locked out.

Across the road from the nursing home was a pub. Who could resist such a well-located place, especially as the walk was good for us! A Scots lad accompanied me. He had been chasing a suspect in Kings Cross across a roof, the roof had collapsed and he had fallen through the building. An Inspector also joined us and told us that he had been sent to the convalescent home because he had undergone a major operation. I'm sure you can understand what it's like, one hour gassing with your pals very quickly turns into two hours, then three and, 'Oh my God, it's eleven o'clock!' We quickly left the pub but because we were still recuperating from our various ailments, we were staggering a little. Who should be waiting for us to return but the sergeant major (whoops, sorry, I mean Matron).

She glared at us. Whether it was her critical eye that caused my friend the Inspector to lose his footing I'll never know for he ended up in her prize rose bush. All three of us were giggling like schoolboys. As we began to make our way in, she shot indoors and, would you believe it, she locked us out! The Scots lad said, 'Don't worry, I unlocked the basement window before we left, just in case we got into any difficulties.' So off we trooped, three decrepit excuses for police officers, and made our way to the basement. We opened the window and I just managed to get through. It was a fairly tight squeeze for me but the Inspector was as broad as he was tall and he had a little more difficulty. In fact, he managed to get only half way through and then found he could not move either forwards or backwards. We were reluctant to push or pull him too much in case we did him some damage. I had no choice but to fetch reinforcements. You can imagine Matron's reaction. Soon, with extra help, the Inspector was released and we all went to bed (without any supper, I might add). The Inspector had to stay in bed for a few days. Later he had to go back to hospital as some of his stitches had torn leaving the wound exposed.

That left myself and the Scotsman. We worked out a plan (well we had to do something to pass the time): if we invited Matron out for a drink maybe we could stay out later. Wrong! She had changed the rules and everyone now had to be in by 9.45pm. In any case, she was not the type to cross the line and associate with her patients. We grudgingly respected her and it is a fact that they certainly don't turn out characters like her nowadays – I don't know whether for better or for worse!

I soon recovered from my operation and was allowed to return to duty, but I had to revert to uniform duties. In the meantime my wife and I had been offered a police house in Hendon and I was transferred to West Hendon Police Station where I was confined to performing light duties for some considerable time.

Chapter Fourteen

WEST HENDON POLICE STATION

It was a hard slog trying to get myself fit again but I managed and I was soon out and about with no more stomach troubles. I was raring to go.

On my first day back on the beat I was sent to the Welsh Harp Lake where the police underwater search unit was recovering stolen jewellery. On the second day they brought up a dead body but, since it was deemed to have been found on Wembley Police's ground, the police officers on that side of the lake had to deal with the corpse.

One evening I was walking along West Hendon Broadway and I couldn't believe my eyes when I saw a man in front of me rattling all the shop door handles. It was obvious that he was looking for an unlocked door in order to break in and steal property. I arrested him and took him to the nick where he was searched and found to be in possession of a variety of door keys, cash register keys and safe keys in his pockets. When I questioned him, he admitted having stolen them from a pub in Hertfordshire. He was charged with the offence of being a suspected person loitering with intent to steal and with the theft of the keys. The case went to Court, where he managed to get away with the suspected person charge but he elected to go for trial on the theft charges. I found him to be very arrogant and he was extremely confident that he would be walking away a free man.

At his trial all the evidence was given and perfectly presented by the witnesses but the Jury decided to find him Not Guilty. I returned his property to him and he laughed at me as I did so. He was escorted to the door of the court and as I watched him step onto the pavement he turned and put two fingers up at me. He was still laughing to himself as he took his road to freedom but I suddenly knew what was going to happen next. Too late! He stepped off the kerb, straight under the wheels of a No.11 bus. I ran to him as fast as I could, frightened at what I might find. I did my best to resuscitate him, but it was no use, he died in my arms. That dreadful incident played on my mind for months afterwards. I wondered what a terrible hand fate had dealt me that evening in West Hendon Broadway. If I had not been there, the man might still be alive today.

I was soon into my old ways of nicking villains and the next one to be arrested was a creep in the car park at the rear of Hendon Court. It was a very dark night, but my eyes had become accustomed to the darkness as I watched a man sitting in a vehicle who looked a little suspicious. He got out of his car and starting peering in all the vehicles. I went over to him and asked him what he was doing. He seemed to be a very educated, polite gentleman. However, when I searched him he had pockets full of ladies' knickers: large pairs, small pairs, all shapes and colours.

I accompanied this gentleman back to his vehicle, which was full of plastic bags. When I looked inside them I saw they were full of ladies' knickers; there seemed to be more knickers than could be found in a branch of Marks & Spencer.

I took him and his vehicle to the nick where the car was searched thoroughly. We found dozens of pornographic books, obscene photographs and more knickers in every conceivable place where he could have put them. He was a resident of Southend-on-Sea and had his own business. It appeared that he travelled long distances up and down the country and used every opportunity to steal ladies knickers off washing lines.

When he was searched he was wearing ladies' knickers and female underwear. It was whilst I searched him that I found a photograph of a very beautiful lady with two neat looking children – they were his wife and family. I had to go to Southend to search his home and I couldn't bring myself to tell his wife what he had done, that was for him to do, but I certainly felt sorry for her.

Then came the task of speaking to all the ladies who had had their knickers stolen. I had to find out the colour and type, etc., and I could have done with Ken Dodd being beside me saying something appropriate, like 'What a lovely day, Missus, for waving your knickers in the air'. Well, perhaps not.

I interviewed all the ladies who had reported their washing missing and some sixty women in the local area came forward. I'm sure they must have thought I was enjoying the task, but I found it very embarrassing and my face must have been getting redder every time I conducted an interview with one of them. All except one of the ladies refused to come to the Station to identify their property. Thank goodness *one* identified her underwear or we might have lost the case.

The thief was ordered by the Magistrate to see a psychiatrist and then he was fined for committing the thefts. I applied to my Guvnor for permission to get rid of the underwear and having got it, I burned the lot. At long last, thank the Lord, I was knickerless.

On the way home from visiting my mother in Australia on a three week holiday, we stopped over in Hong Kong and I bought one of those new fangled digital watches where you press buttons and the time lights up then goes out again, leaving a black face. (Well they were new fangled at the time but now it seems as though digital watches have always been around.)

My first job when I got back to West Hendon was a burglary where stolen items were being fenced in Chapel Street Market. I went there and on an antique stall I recognised some of the pieces that had been stolen in the robbery. I took them and the seller to the nick. The seller gave me the name of the person who had sold the items to her and it did not take too much detective work to trace the person and arrest him for burglary.

Quite some time passed before the case was heard at St Albans Crown Court and I was required to give evidence. As I sat in the waiting area of the court for the case to be called, the burglar asked me what time it was. I lifted my arm and pressed the button on my watch and told him it was 10.35pm. The light had showed the time and then gone out, leaving just the black face of the watch as I lowered my arm.

The burglar sat in amazement trying to puzzle it out and said, 'Tell me Sir, how can you tell the time with that watch of yours – the face is all black?' I replied, 'I've got x-ray eyes, how do you think I caught you?' The funny thing is, he actually believed me! When he was asked in Court if he pleaded guilty or not guilty, he replied, 'Guilty, Sir'. But before then he had had no intention of pleading guilty!

Another con trick I pulled was on an Irish lad who had stopped his lorry on the highway and was loading it with paving stones which obviously were not his property. A lady who had been watching him rang through to the Station and gave me the index number of his vehicle. I carried out an owner check and within three seconds I had his name and address.

I went straight around to his house and spoke to his wife who informed me that her husband was on his way home. She invited me in and made me a cup of tea. A few minutes later, her husband arrived with the lorry loaded with slabs. I told him who I was and why I was there and arrested him. He was bewildered and wanted to know how it was that he had stolen the slabs and come straight home, only to find me already there waiting to arrest him. I told him I was psychic and that I could see things before they actually happened.

He asked me what would happen at Court and I told him he would be fined £40 plus costs. We went to Hendon Crown Court and when the evidence was heard the Magistrate said 'Fined £40 plus costs.' As I took him down to pay his debts he said, 'I see what you mean, you are psychic!'

My wife and I went out for a meal in a pub and as we sat down in the lounge we noticed that the landlord and landlady were drunk and argumentative and both were shouting very loudly. Suddenly the landlady hit her husband on the back of the head with an object (I couldn't see what it was) before leaping over the bar and running round to the other bar, followed by her husband. She then ran back into the lounge bar, leapt over the counter as before, and round and round they went. After about six circuits, the landlord stopped and hid beneath the bar. As his wife leapt the bar for the final time, he jumped up and smacked her on top of the head with a bottle, splitting her head open. She lay there on the ground, blood pouring from her wound. My wife and I stopped the flow of blood and called for an ambulance. Then police arrived. I told them what I'd seen and everyone burst out laughing when I said, 'The beer's bloody horrible, but the cabaret was marvellous.'

So much for a nice relaxing meal with my wife! We went home after the cabaret and cooked a meal in the peace of our own home.

I went to this same pub one lunchtime to have a snack. The pub was close to the where the Ml was being constructed and was used by the construction workers. It was pouring with rain and the pub was full of customers. Six or seven construction workers entered the pub. They'd been paid off because of the weather. They ordered whiskys, brandies and rums but when the landlord brought them their drinks they said, 'No not glasses, bottles', so the landlord granted them their request.

I left the pub but called in later at the end of the day and saw the same men still drinking from bottles and sitting at the same table. The landlord told me that they had spent over £600 on drinks. I was having a peaceful pint and heard the men start up a singing contest. The landlady ran over to them, took away their drinks and threw the men out onto the street. I told her I thought she was being a bit harsh on them after they had spent all that money, but she replied, 'They were broke anyway, and we have a no singing licence.'

Funny old world, isn't it?

Brent Cross Shopping Centre had just been completed. It was one of the first gigantic shopping malls in North London, situated between Golders Green and Hendon. No sooner was the opening ceremony over than the villains moved in – pickpockets, shoplifters and drug dealers. Arrests were made for all these offences and more. The Centre became so well known that people came from South America, Mexico, Africa and Spain and many other countries, simply to steal. There were rich pickings to be had.

On one occasion, I was called to arrest a group of people who had been held on suspicion of stealing goods. None of them could speak a word of English so we took them off to the nick in the van. The group included males and females. Interpreters were brought in and it was found that the group came from three of the countries mentioned above, so they were banged up whilst we went to search their temporary accommodation. Their rooms were like Aladdin's Cave, stocked high with all manner of goods, including recording equipment.

When the suspects were questioned, they told us that it was well known that it was easy to shoplift in England – and by the look of their rooms it was true! They assured us that this was the main reason they had come to the United Kingdom. How on earth does someone walk out of a shop with a television without paying for it?

Eventually the case went to court and the thieves were fined. It may not surprise you to know that they had plenty of money to pay the fines.

It was not long before the shoplifters were back to their old tricks and they soon made up the money (and more besides) that they had forked out to pay their fines. They were not deported and they are probably still carrying out their scams in other shopping centres in this country. The law of averages says that thieves get caught only one in twenty times. No wonder they say that this country is a soft touch.

On another day, I drove my car into this same shopping centre, when a man walked straight out in front of me. I slammed on the brakes and just managed to stop in time. My son was in the car with me. I parked the vehicle and was walking out of the car park when another man said to me, 'Be careful, that man who walked in front of you is waiting behind the pillar with his car's jack handle.' Just then two burly security guards came and grabbed me and belted me, so I told them they were both under arrest for assaulting a police officer. The man who had walked in front of my car then belted me and ran off.

I took the two security guards to their office and told their manager what had happened. He was speechless after hearing that they had let my assailant escape and that the guards were now under arrest. The guards stood with their mouths open, their 'bottle' had completely gone. The Duty Inspector arrived and, after some discussion, we agreed that they should be released. They claimed that they had only been doing their job.

That was not the end of this story. I was at home one day when I saw the dustmen coming along the road emptying the bins. I watched them, absentmindedly. As one of the men came to collect my bin I realised it was the very man who had run away from the car park after he had belted me. I opened my back door and as he walked in to get the bin I grabbed him. He jumped a mile at the sight of me and dropped the bin. I gave him a warning – for the future.

As we say in the Job, 'There's always another day.'

I was on duty in Hendon Central when an accident happened between two cars, one containing two Jewish women and the other an Arab. Apparently what had happened was that the two ladies, who were sisters, had ran into the Arab's car which was parked at the kerb and he had come out of his office and started an almighty row. I thought, I don't need this, it's the Suez Crisis all over again. (I'd got a medal from the first one, I didn't need one for this.) The two women were knocking hell out of the Arab. He fell to the ground and they jumped on him. I pulled them off and told them to calm down or they would be arrested. They both said, 'He's only an Arab.' This was now becoming an international incident.

I sent the Arab back into his office and took the ladies' details and sent them home, intending to visit them later. I then dealt with the Arab. Having taken his statement, I called on the Jewish ladies at their home and took their statements over a nice pot of tea. Unfortunately, as well as getting their statements I was given a lecture on the history of the Jewish nation, from Genesis right through to the present day. I tried to remain attentive but if I didn't show that I was listening and nodding in the right place then I got an ear bashing.

However, it all ended well. I was invited to call in for a cup of tea any time I was in the area – and I got a similar invitation from the Arab.

I'll be a diplomat for the United Nations yet!

I was returning to the nick having completed observation duty in the Mill Hill area and was passing through Burnt Oak when I spotted Charlie Burns (I've changed his name). Charlie was well known to local coppers.

I made a note of the time and when I got back at the nick I recorded the 'sighting' in the Collator's Book.

I had forgotten about the incident until Detective Inspector McAdam sent for me and said, 'Do you remember the Wembley Bank Robbery?' I replied that I did. He went on to ask if I remembered seeing Charlie Burns in the Burnt Oak area and then noting the fact in the Collator's Book. Again I replied that I did and took out my pocket book and showed him the relevant entry. Detective Inspector McAdam then said, 'Good, the robbery occurred twenty-five minutes before you saw him. We have brought him in for questioning but he denies the offence because he states that he was over one hundred miles away at the time. He also says he has witnesses to prove it.' My reply was that he must have been lying.

Charlie was being held at Wembley Police Station and when my testimony came to light he was charged with committing the robbery and sent to prison for a good many years.

Observation and a keen eye is the main object of good police work, as I remembered on another occasion. I was in Hendon Central when I saw a man dressed in leathers and a crash helmet riding a motorcycle. A gut reaction told me something was not quite right so I made a note of the registration number of the motorbike together with a brief description of the rider.

I saw the same man in the same place, at the same time the following week, so again I wrote it all down. I also took a look around on this occasion and after a little while a security van drew up outside the bank. I recorded all the facts and later transferred my findings into the Collator's records.

I went to the same location a week later. This time the man in question was nowhere to be seen. However, the security van arrived at the same time as the previous week.

Well, needless to say, on the fourth week, just as the security van was delivering money, four men with shotguns carried out a raid. The raiders injured one of the guards and got away with thousands of pounds in a mini van. They drove the wrong way down the A41 towards the Brent flyover, then careered through a pedestrian under-pass, out the other side and dumped the van. They made good their escape in a get-away car.

The first thing I did on hearing this news was to run a check on the motorbike and the man in the leathers I'd seen in Hendon Central. It transpired that he was a well known villain, who was on bail for another robbery in the City, and part of his bail conditions were that he should report to Islington nick daily at 1pm.

I rang the nick and spoke to the Station officer and asked what time he had reported to the nick on the day of our robbery. The answer was not what I wanted to hear. He said 5 minutes after our robbery.

I decided not to leave it at this, so I requested that a Traffic Patrol motorcyclist drive from Hendon Central to Islington in order to see what time it would take. It was 30 minutes – far too long. I asked him to try again, and then again. He got it down to 25 minutes, and his fastest time was 19 minutes. But this was still no good as it was obviously impossible for our suspect to be in two places at the same time.

Still unsatisfied, I went to Islington nick and examined the reporting book. The sergeant on duty, realising my concern, advised me to speak to the officer who actually recorded his time. This I did.

He told me: 'Yes, I remember that day, he was about 30 minutes late. His excuse was that he was at the hospital looking after his dying mother and didn't wish to leave her. The villain had gone on to ask if, on this one occasion, he (the officer) would forget that he was late and record the time as 1pm as normal. This was duly done.

I checked out the story about his dying mother, and found that she was alive and well, living in a lovely home he had no doubt bought for her out of his ill-gotten gains. The word that came to my mind was 'Gotcher'.

I took a quick statement from the officer and then headed straight to D.I. McAdam at West Hendon to report my findings. He listened to my story and made arrangements to have my villain arrested. (It also came to light that our man had left his motorcycle at Brent Cross and drove as fast as he could to report to Islington.)

Our next job was to contact the Flying Squad and arrange for them to raid numerous addresses. This happened early the following morning at 2.30am, and they were issued with fire-arms for the occasion.

The raids were successful, five of the gang were arrested for the robbery and a lot of money was recovered. A bundle of money was recovered from a most unusual hiding place – under a baby who was sleeping in her cot!

When all the confiscated articles had been recorded we found that this particular gang were connected with numerous robberies in other parts of the country.

The paper work was completed and it stood in a pile about 6 feet high. The gang were committed for trial at the Old Bailey.

The stolen money, incidently, was specially dyed so that it couldn't be spent. One thing I remember clearly about this case was that some time later, as we were sitting in the Old Bailey, D.I. McAdam casually asked me where the money was. Well, *I* hadn't got it! Panic set in – but luck was on our side that day. I raced back to West Hendon nick and there it sat, just where he had left it, on his desk, all £20,000 of it.

I made it back to Court just in time to see the gang found guilty and and to receive sentences from 12 to 20 years imprisonment.

At about this time D.I. McAdam sent for me and said 'I've seen your reports in the Collator's records; you have done another good job. Will you come back in the CID, we need you.'

I thought about his request but decided to decline the offer. However I learnt that he had already spoken to the Superintendent and arranged for me to be on loan to the CID as the office manager of the Robbery Squad. So when I refused he was astonished, this really messed up his plans. So he told me to go away and think about it.

It didn't take long for me to agree.

One evening I was driving home along the North Circular Road. It was pelting with rain and the road was in a mess as contractors were altering the lay-out. Suddenly the traffic came to an immediate standstill. I could see that an accident had just occurred so I pulled onto the side of the road and went to see if there was anything I could do to help.

Two cars had collided head on (visibility was very bad due to the driving rain). I saw two officers dealing with the accident but sadly it was obvious that both the drivers and all the passengers had died on impact. Eventually all the bodies were removed by the fire brigade and the mess of mangled metal was taken away for forensic tests. The road was now clearing well and everyone was able to continue on their journeys home.

As I left the scene of the accident I heard something – it sounded like a cat whining. I went with another officer to investigate. The sound was coming from a blackthorn tree thick with thorns. I must admit I don't like cats at the best of time, but I could not be so cruel as to walk away. It was obvious that someone had to get the cat down. I thought that it might have been in one of the cars and that it was the only survivor from the wreckage.

The fire brigade had already left the scene so I volunteered to climb the tree. I broke off some of the lower branches and inched my way steadily up, cursing every time I got a thorn in my hand or leg. It wasn't long before I had managed to rip my trousers on a particularly sharp branch.

Up I went, onwards and upwards, when all of a sudden, I let out such a yell that the other officer, concerned for my well being, asked, 'What's up?' I couldn't believe my eyes, it was a lovely baby wrapped in a shawl and it was gurgling away. I was reminded of the nursery rhyme 'Rock-a-bye baby, on the tree top.' How on earth had the baby got up the tree! I picked it up carefully, made my way carefully down the tree and passed it as gently as I could to the officer waiting below. Tears welled up in my eyes when I realised that it had been thrown clear of the car through the windscreen and up into the tree. It looked in perfect condition. The baby was taken to hospital for a thorough health check and was indeed found to be in good health. It was taken into temporary care and I never heard what happened subsequently.

God had certainly looked after that little baby that night.

I had been at West Hendon Police Station for some time when I received a message from my old Detective Inspector at Chelsea inviting me to their Christmas Party. Never one to pass up on an invitation, I straight away replied that wild horses would not keep me away from this 'do'.

The night arrived and we arranged to meet at a certain pub in the Fulham Road where we used to drink with the actor Dudley Sutton, who played the part of Tinker in the television programme *Lovejoy*. He wasn't there that evening, but I did recognise the barman who I knew was wanted all over North London for dozens of thefts and I had been looking for him for some time. As most of his crimes had been committed whilst he was working in pubs, I informed the DI who I knew was a friend of the landlord of the pub. He beckoned a young officer over and told him to get a uniform police officer to come to the pub and arrest the wanted man.

The DI then took the landlord to one side and told him what was going to happen and just as the landlord and DI came out of the back office some uniform officers arrived. The barman spotted them and made a quick dash for the door, but he was stopped in his tracks and arrested. The barman said to me, 'I recognised you, but I thought you hadn't recognised me.'

He was taken to Chelsea nick and later was transferred to Golders Green nick where he was charged with fraud, false accounting and theft from pubs, i.e. by short-changing customers and stealing from the cash tills. At court, 70 other offences were taken into consideration.

The DI introduced me to the landlord, who thanked me for saving his takings. He added that his takings had already started to go down since employing the barman. The landlord bought us both a drink and later we went on to the Christmas party that was being held at Chelsea Fire Station. My old DI then gave me a bottle of vodka as a Christmas present for assisting in this case.

Looking back, as police officers we were never off duty and we were always on the lookout for criminals. Another one bites the dust.

As I said earlier, DI McAdam had asked me to go back into the CID. After thinking about it long and hard I decided to go for it and filled out my application form. It was accepted immediately without the formality of an interview, with a posting to Golders Green.

I remember as a child my father telling me that if I didn't learn at school, I'd be sweeping the streets for the rest of my life. I never liked school and needed lots of encouragement (including the stick) to persuade me to attend every day and to do as I was told. The funny thing is that now I was 'sweeping the streets' by attempting to keep them free of criminals while I tried to be a good and honest copper.

There was a lot of cleaning still to be done, so when I arrived at Golders Green Police Station I went back to the police college at Hendon on the CID course.

The Criminal Investigation Course was designed to teach us to become thief-takers. The college was based in a building that had been recently built and everything was state of the art. It contained an auditorium for lectures where all the top scientists, hand writing experts, pathologists and experts in many other fields were able to offer their advice to enable us to become first class police officers.

We covered every aspect of the law and acted out scenes of crimes, murder, assaults etc. and we had home studies until we learned the law inside out, or as has been said, we could recite it backwards. It was learn, cram, learn, cram and cram some more. On a Wednesday, learning was taboo because it was sports day and the evening was kept free for dining out and a heavy drinking session.

One Wednesday night we all went out on the town to local pubs and clubs until we got home and collapsed in our beds. I woke up the following day and saw with horror that it was ten o'clock in the morning! I leapt out of bed and got into the lecture room in ten minutes flat. I said to the Instructor, 'Sorry I'm late, Sir, I missed the bus.' He told me to sit down. At the bell for mid-morning break (which was not too long afterwards) I made my way out of the room, very quickly. On my return, the instructor called me over and said, 'Beard, come out here, you only live thirty yards from this room, what do you mean by saying that you missed the bus?' I replied, 'I thought you knew Sir that I lived across the road.' He was not a happy bunny and yelled at me, 'Right, that's deception, learn that part of the law tonight and it will make you think next time you decide to deceive me.'

I had the most terrible night trying to learn this piece of law parrot fashion in addition to my other homework which, believe me, was considerable. I stayed up all night. When I entered the classroom the following morning, the Instructor asked me if I had learned the law. I told him, 'The best I could, sir.' He didn't ask me to repeat it (Phew!)

As time passed, I got used to the weekly examinations at junior and intermediate level. I also visited scenes of crime with other officers in the class who were from other parts of the country as well as Ireland and Wales.

At one stage, we were each given a subject to lecture on to the whole class. I chose Terrorism. I begged and borrowed all the literature I could lay my hands on about the subject and studied so much at night that I certainly didn't need rocking to sleep. Over the next few days, everyone gave a lecture except me. I hoped that they had forgotten me, but I was wrong. One day we were all paraded and told to report to the main auditorium. When we arrived, I noticed that the four front rows were empty but that the rest of the seats filled up in quick succession. I was then called up to the front and told to be ready to give my lecture to the people assembled in the auditorium.

I stood on the stage and looked down at the sea of faces. My bottle went. 'Lord, help me,' I thought to myself. There were hundreds of faces watching me. As I looked down I noticed that the four front rows were filling up with senior officers, senior police college officers, the Commissioner, Members of Parliaments, Chief Constables, Judges and Lawyers. When they were all seated I wondered what they were waiting for. My knees started to tremble and turned to jelly. I then realised that they were waiting for me to begin my lecture!

I made a stuttering start. However, I had done so much research that I knew my chosen subject backwards and soon fell into a kind of rhythm, the confidence flowing back into my body. The words just seemed to come out and they seemed to be making sense. I became so engrossed in my lecture that I was no longer was aware of the sea of faces and I poured my heart into my talk.

I had dates, times and incidents of all the terrorist activities that had taken place in Ireland, India, Cyprus, Palestine, Germany and the French occupied countries. I spent some time talking about EOKA in Cyprus and General Grevas. Then I moved on to India and to the period when Ghandi had been active. I spoke about the Irish Republican Army and about the Commonwealth Countries.

I completed my talk, which had lasted for about two hours, and went to step down off the stage to return to my seat. The applause that met me as I left the stage was extremely noisy and the audience clapped for some time. When it was announced that it was time for a break I knew I could do with a drink.

I relaxed too much during the break because afterwards I was called back up to the rostrum and I was in a worse state than I had been previously. I thought I had finished but no, it was question time. Questions came thick and fast and some came from my mates (who were taking the Micky), and an hour later my session came to an end. This time I received a standing ovation and my Inspector told me that my lecture was one of the best he had ever heard.

More applause followed and I was eventually able to return to my seat (my head by this time was ten times bigger than when I had begun). I wished that my two original tutors (Air Marshal of the RAF, Sir Ivor Broom and Group Captain Burberry) could have been there on that day because it was when I was in the RAF that these two had set me on my road to education at the age of eighteen. If they had been there to listen to my lecture, my day would have been complete.

Photographs taken, final examinations passed, goodbyes having been said, we returned to our respective Forces and to our respective Stations. I made my way back to Golders Green and two weeks passed before I learned the results of the course. I had passed with flying colours. I was looking forward to my chosen way of life.

Chapter Fifteen

A COPPER'S LOT IS A HAPPY ONE

I soon got down to work again at Golders Green. The first job I had to do was to question a fourteen-year old boy about the theft of some cash. He already had 114 previous convictions. (One for the record books, I would have thought.)

I went to his house with another officer to investigate yet another of the boy's little scams. The modus operandi of his family was that they would all enter a shop (in this case Woolworth's). One member of the family would steal a pair of scissors and cut the cord holding the till keys hanging from an assistant's waistband. Meanwhile, another member of the family, usually the fourteen-year old boy, caught the keys before they hit the floor. The keys were then passed on to the mother or father who would go to the unattended till and relieve it of all its cash. Then they would all decamp. However, now and again one or more of them got caught.

The members of this family were not particularly bright but whatever was said about them they had enough intelligence to work out methods of crime like this. None of the family ever worked and they always had the best things in life. (So who are the thick ones one might ask?)

The boy admitted the offence and off to court we went yet again. All he got was a slap on the wrist (I know, I know, we're not allowed to do this, are we?) and he was given a Conditional Discharge for the 115th time. What a complete waste of everyone's time and effort. However, his time was to come. After committing a few more offences he was eventually sent to an approved school, then to Borstal, and finally to prison. (But there again, criminals are so well looked after in prison that their sentences are little more than a rest period before they get out and offend again.)

We always said he had a key job!

●

A colleague and I had to go to Manchester by train to collect a prisoner. We were expected to do the journey there and back in one day in order to save the taxpayers' money. So Detective Constable Williams and I caught an early express out of Euston Station and rattled off in the direction of the big city.

We were mulling over a can of beer in the refreshment bar watching the world go by whilst travelling through Staffordshire, when there was an almighty BANG!, followed by CRASH!, SMASH!, and WALLOP! The cans were thrown one way and we another, people were scattered all over the floor, and the refreshment bar was wrecked. One thing was definite, we weren't going anywhere for a while.

DC Williams and I sat for ages whilst the rail experts toured the train seeking out the injured. They told us that our train had rammed a train in front that had been conveying new motorcars from the Midlands to Liverpool Docks. The line was covered in cars and wreckage.

It took six hours to clear away the mess and by this time it was four o'clock in the afternoon. Meanwhile, messages were sent from Manchester to Golders Green Police Station enquiring as to the whereabouts of the officers they were expecting. People at the nick were getting worried and thought that we had overslept on the train and were now in John O'Groats or some such place. No one was aware that we had been involved in a train crash, nor had they thought to check! We weren't worried because we had our beer and food – which to our delight was now complimentary – but it was a big disappointment to us when we found out that we had drunk the bar dry!

Eventually, eight hours after the crash, the train was allowed to move but we were only pushed to the next main station, from where we had a very slow journey to Manchester. By the time we arrived at our destination, we were extremely tired and hungry. We were met by local police officers and as there were no more trains leaving that day they took us out for a meal and arranged for us to stay overnight at a very cosy guesthouse. The following day we collected our prisoner and made our way back to London. This time the journey was much quicker than the previous day's.

After the prisoner had been charged and put in a cell for the night, we heard our Guvnor shout, 'Williams, Beard, my office, now!' We made our way to his office not knowing what to expect. Well, we got a right royal rollicking for staying overnight and for claiming expenses for a meal and a bed for the night. Even though we explained that we had been involved in a train crash and delayed for ten hours, it made little difference. 'You should have used your brains and got to Manchester by some other means, then got back here on time as you were instructed.' I could not stop myself saying, 'What, walk all the way on the bloody train lines?'

You just can't please some people can you?

I was on patrol with DC Brian Lawrence in the CID car as a result of all the burglaries that had been committed in the garden suburb of Hampstead and as we were cruising round we got a call from Information Room at Scotland Yard: 'Sierra Golf Five, men acting suspiciously at the rear of a house in Cricklewood Lane.'

We sped off towards the venue through Golders Green and as we were going down a hill the front offside wheel of our car hit the central reservation. The car flipped over and we slid quite a long way on the roof, sparks flying and petrol leaking all over the road. How we didn't catch fire I'll never know. I was upside down and couldn't get out until I was released by a passing police constable, who called an ambulance which took us to hospital. (Police rules require that if an officer receives any injury or knock on the head he must go to hospital.) We were checked over and found to be unhurt, so we were sent back to the nick.

Incidentally, the men who were 'acting suspiciously' in Cricklewood Lane were refuse collectors, would you believe, making their weekly call.

And we managed to get another rollicking from the Guvnor!

One dark winter's evening, the Guvnor dumped a piece of paper on my desk. I lazily glanced at it and said, 'Why can't night duty deal with this?' He replied, 'Just get on with it,' so I picked up the piece of paper and set off, moaning under my breath because I had already been on duty for ten hours. It was approximately ten-thirty. I read the piece of paper on which was written, '*Allegation of rape in a block of flats.*' It also gave the address and the name of the informant. I knew just how long these jobs could take and I felt very aggrieved that one of the officers on the night duty shift had not been given this one to do. What made matters worse was that it was during the time that we were subjected to frequent power cuts due to the strikes that were taking place at the time.

I drove my car to the scene and saw the informant who told me that the girl who had been raped lived on the top floor of the block of flats. (Isn't it always the top floor when there is no lift working?) Everywhere was in complete and utter darkness and the flats were deserted. By this time I had been joined by a WPC who was on night duty.

We talked to each other in a breathless fashion as we plodded up from one step to the next. It was a marathon trek to the top. In the darkness I fell over a child's bicycle which had been left on the landing. The WPC laughed and said, 'No time to lie down on the job, Jim.'

At last we got to the door of the girl's flat and banged on it. It soon opened and in we went. We saw a girl sitting on a sofa crying softly. In between sobs she said, 'I've been raped by a man in his car.' I was shocked because I realised that I knew the girl. She worked in a local pub as a barmaid. Unfortunately, she had a reputation for going home with different boyfriends, but this was irrelevant and I vowed to make sure that, regardless of her reputation, she was going to get every support and that the matter would be fully investigated.

I began by going through the normal procedure for this type of crime. I asked her, 'Are you still wearing the same clothes you wore when the crime was committed?' She said she was. 'Have you washed or had a bath?' I asked. She shook her head and said no. A little while later she told the WPC the full story, which was that when she finished work at the pub she was chatted up by a gypsy who subsequently agreed to run her home. However, instead of doing so he abducted her and drove her to a lonely spot in the countryside where he tore her clothing off her and raped her.

I asked the WPC to take her upstairs to get some fresh clothing for her to change into after the relevant examinations had been made. The WPC then escorted the victim to the police doctor in Highgate who was an expert in such cases for a complete check up and for the normal tests to be carried out. After that, I carefully placed all the clothes she had been wearing at the time of the incident into plastic bags and labelled them. Notes were taken meticulously on her condition, her wounds, tears to her clothing and any other abnormality. Once all the necessary procedures had been completed, I told the girl to shower and get changed. Then we went to the Police Station where a formal statement was taken, specimens were labelled ready for the laboratory and reports were prepared.

We were now armed with all the evidence. No stone was left unturned and eventually we brought in the suspect. By this time it was half past four in the morning and the Detective Inspector had arrived at the Station. I was sent home to have a meal, a very short catnap, and a bath. I later found myself back at the Station looking at the grubby looking individual who had been accused of rape and abduction.

The suspect was escorted to Court and remanded in custody to await trial. When the case was dealt with he was found Not Guilty of abduction but Guilty of rape and duly punished for this terrible crime.

Girls who are subject to such terrible ordeals where their clothes are ripped off and they are left badly injured, both physically and mentally, go through years of hell and suffer long after the rapist is freed. Some victims never return to normal life and whatever their background they don't deserve to be raped. What happens to them afterwards, no one knows and some people don't seem to care. Even worse is that some young girls never tell anyone that they have been raped because they fear having to give evidence at court and cannot face the prospect of being cross examined by the rapist's barrister. They suffer in silence forever.

As a police officer, I've seen dozens of these girls in my time and in all the situations I have mentioned, we as police officers never had time to think of ourselves. We were there to serve and to be completely devoted to bringing criminals to justice, however much time and effort it took.

Time passes on and I'd just had another long day, working from nine o'clock in the morning to eleven o'clock at night. As I was about to go home, the boss man told us that he wished to take us all to a night club in Golders Green for a quick drink before we all went off duty. (Or at least that's what we thought.)

I was so tired by this time that I was holding on to my drink and wondering how I could do a quick vanishing act without the Guvnor knowing. But one did not do so without his say so. Andy Patrick then walked in and said, 'The Superintendent wants everyone back at the nick.' Off we all went back to the Station where we were informed that a robbery had occurred at the home of Lieutenant Colonel Noonpakdee, an Attaché at the Thai Embassy in London.

The story was as follows. A gang had burst into his home and bound and gagged him and his family. They were robbed and valuables were taken from the house. Apparently, the Attaché had been mistaken for the owner of a chinese restaurant and so the gang were looking for the restaurant takings at the wrong house. When they could find no money, they took the Lieutenant Colonel's gold Buddha and all his gold medals. The King of Thailand had presented the gold medals to the Lieutenant Colonel and he dreaded the thought of returning to Thailand to report their loss because it was a very serious matter for which he could be beheaded. He was a very worried man.

We worked through the night and the next day, taking statements, conducting interviews, and making enquiries. Three nights after the robbery had occurred, another took place at the Chinese Garden restaurant in the West End. A revolver was pointed at the owner but it didn't go off. Again the robber tried to shoot him but he was unable to get the gun to work, so he threw it at the owner before drawing a knife and stabbing him instead.

The owner of the restaurant lost a lot of blood but he survived. It did not take long to tie both crimes in with each other. When the victim recovered he was able to give us a description of the gang which was made up of Chinese and white men. Unfortunately, we had nothing else to go on at that stage.

We then received information about a similar robbery in Swansea in South Wales, in which a Chinese gang had been involved. They got away in a red Datsun car and though it was a long shot I decided to take it upon myself to ring the only two garages in London that rented out Datsuns and ask if they had hired out any of their vehicles to Chinese men recently. *Bingo*! A garage in Wembley had rented a red Datsun to three Chinese men a month previously. In addition, the staff were able to tell me that the car must have been taken to the West Country because they had received a summons in respect of the car alleging that the driver had committed a speeding offence.

I later learned that the gun the gang of robbers had used at the Chinese Garden restaurant had been tested and it was capable of being fired.

Now, armed with the names and addresses of the gang, we went to the house of the first, an Australian, who lived in Reading. We searched it and found explosives, guns and ammunition making equipment, and a quantity of drugs.

The Australian was brought to the nick and held there pending further enquiries. He was later charged and he gave us the address in Battersea of an accomplice. We paid a visit to this gentleman's house and found the gold Buddha that had been taken on the night of the robbery at Lieutenant Noonpakdee's house. He too was promptly arrested and charged.

Early the next morning, all the streets round an address that we'd been given for four other Chinese men were sealed off. We drew our weapons and made our way to their rented apartment. The caretaker got an awful fright when he saw us, especially since he had just woken up. Once he had calmed down, he gave us the keys to the suspects' rooms. Detective Superintendent Snodgrass and I quietly entered one of the rooms. Two Chinese males were asleep on the bed. The Superintendent went to one side of the bed and I went round to the other. Mr Snodgrass then mouthed the word 'Now' and at his signal we both stuck our guns into their necks and before they knew it the men were handcuffed.

The same thing took place in the second apartment. All four men were taken to the Station and both apartments were thoroughly (and I mean thoroughly) searched. We found £1,000,000 worth of heroin and two of the Lieutenant Colonel's medals. One officer was left to guard the premises and we took all the goodies to the nick.

Later, a police constable radioed that he had detained a young Chinese girl who had come to the flats to see her boyfriend. She was arrested and brought to the Station where her keys were taken and I was assigned to search her flat. Whilst searching it I found a quantity of heroin and when I looked in her dressing table I found the other medals belonging to Lieutenant Colonel Noonpakdee. They had been painstakingly sewn into the inner lining of the girl's knickers. (Can't anyone free me of these troublesome knickers?) I also found items stolen in the Swansea robbery.

Further arrests were made after observation was kept on the block of flats where the four suspects lived and information revealed that all the arrested men were members of Triad gangs.

Lieutenant Colonel Noonpakdee came to the Station and when I told him that we had found his medals he got down and kissed my feet. Then he shook my hand and invited all the members of the Squad to his house for a party that night to celebrate the good work. After the party, we went on to the Playboy Club. The Lieutenant Colonel gave us some money to gamble with at the tables. I had a very good win, which I decided to donate to a Police Charity.

The gang members went for trial at the Old Bailey where between them they were given over 200 years imprisonment. The Judge commended all concerned and we received a Commissioner's Commendation.

This case appeared on billboards and in newspapers around the world. My mother who was in the Far East at the time on her way to visit me saw the papers and brought them with her.

Another street cleaning job done.

My first job with the Burglary Squad found me on observation duty near a car park in Edgware. I saw a man walk into the car park and he seemed to be looking in all the cars. I watched as he bobbed and weaved around one car and then got down underneath another. He then went round the first car again and repeated the operation. This went on for quite some time and I thought that he was either trying to steal a car or steal from a car.

He continued bobbing about as I walked up to him to arrest him on the evidence that I'd seen. I said to him, 'I'm a police officer...', but that was as far as I got because I recognised him as Frank Williams who played the part of the Vicar in the television show *Dad's Army*. The reason why he was bobbing about was because there was an injured pigeon hiding under the cars and he was trying to catch it to take it to a vet.

I summoned my mates on the Burglary Squad (or should I say Flying Squad?) We soon rounded up Frank's pigeon, which was sent on its way to the vet.

I now know how the Flying Squad got its name.

For some weeks, contractors' equipment was going missing from building sites in North London. We were instructed to carry out observations but could never see anything or catch anyone.

The stolen gear included JCBs, tractors, bulldozers, and generators. We contacted all our 'snouts' but they came up with nothing until one day an informant rang to tell us that the thief was a contractor himself who was shipping the equipment to Ireland.

I put out an all ports warning to look out for the equipment, which was big enough to be noticed on its way abroad. (We never counted on the equipment being dismantled before being packed in cases and then shipped.)

As a last ditch attempt, we decided to raid the contractor at his yard in Cricklewood. We went to the venue and after arriving and parking the car we walked up the gravel drive and knocked at the door. We showed him the warrant and searched his house. Only one item of stolen property was found, but there was an engine on a bench awaiting repair. As we walked down the drive, I thought the gravel was exceptionally deep so a few of us decided to find the reason why. We got four shovels and told the contractor and his men to start digging. They reluctantly dug down until the top of a tractor came into view. Further down, more of the tractor appeared until the whole of it was showing. At that moment a lorry loaded with packing cases arrived.

We then twigged it – the disposal of the stolen equipment had baffled us for a year but now everything fell into place. The engine on the bench had been stolen and it was part of a tractor that had been shipped weeks ago. The contractor was waiting for packing cases to be delivered to enable them to ship out other stolen equipment.

A prison sentence was passed on the contractor and his men. What a way to earn money, sheer greed.

They were soon free to start again elsewhere.

Back on the car patrol with my old friend Fred Arnold, the father of three lovely girls and the husband of a loving wife. Fred and his brother, both good coppers, had a hard start in life as orphans. They had lived in an orphanage and had suffered great hardship. Fred was about six feet six inches tall and he would look down at us and take the Mickey about our lack of height. He would say things like, 'Where do you buy your clothes, Mothercare?' But we took his teasing in good spirit and I admired him, especially as he saved my bacon a few times.

A warrant of arrest fell on Fred's desk one day. The warrant was for the arrest of a man in Cricklewood for non-payment of rates. Off we went to the wanted man's address and when the culprit came to the door in answer to our knock he was promptly arrested and taken straight to the Court at Hendon to appear that afternoon. We had to give evidence of arrest. He had two people with him, one was his solicitor and the other was from the Department of Social Security. The Social Security guy went into the witness box and told the Magistrate that the Department would pay the man's rates. The man was given seven days to pay and he was released.

Seven days passed and Fred again got a warrant of arrest on his desk. It was for the same man for the same offence. We wondered if there had been some mistake but in any case we set off again and arrested our friend. Again we accompanied him to Court, where he appeared before the same Magistrate. The man from the Department of Social Security was also there. The arrested man told the Court that he had been paid the money by the DSS but he had promptly spent it. We were shocked when the DSS representative told the Court that they would again pay the money on the man's behalf. We looked at each other with disgust at the thought of a Government Department wasting taxpayers' money in that way. The Magistrate quite rightly made an order that the money must be paid direct to the Court.

It had cost the taxpayers of this country a great deal of money to bring the case to Court and to pay the rates twice over. But sadly nothing ever seems to be done to right this kind of wrong.

It was eleven o'clock at night and I was sitting at my desk when the telephone rang. It was my snout (informant) who told me that a load of television sets had just been delivered to a shop near his house. I obtained a search warrant from the local magistrate who asked if his daughter could accompany me. The Chief Inspector agreed and a little while later the girl arrived at the nick in her father's Rolls Royce.

The shop was in darkness when we arrived in the Magistrate's roller.

We hammered the door down so that there was an element of surprise. The owner lived above the shop and he soon came down, whereupon we showed him the search warrant. We began the search and soon found twenty brand new television sets. I asked him where he had got them from and he admitted that they had been stolen. He gave us the names and addresses of the thieves. He went on to say that he was running a business selling and renting television sets and the plan had been that these sets would have been rented out to customers. Early the next morning we went to the thieves' addresses and after breaking in we found them in bed. They were allowed time to get dressed before being taken to the Police Station.

The story they told amazed us all. They said that they had gone into a television shop in the Kings Cross area. An insurance scam had been devised between the owner of the shop and the thieves in which the thieves would steal the television sets and then the owner would claim the cost of replacing them from the insurance company.

The plan was ingenious. They knocked down the inside of the double-thickness back wall one afternoon and took just a couple of bricks out of the outside wall. The shop backed onto wasteland. When it got dark, the gang backed their van up to the rear wall and then continued to remove the outside bricks. The rest was easy, the television sets were taken straight out of the shop and into the van where a willing accomplice was waiting to receive them.

Both shopkeepers were arrested and sent to prison, they lost their livelihoods and were blacklisted by the insurance companies. The thieves were fined but were free to try again. And try again they did.

One night I was on duty when I saw a new Mercedes car parked against the kerb with the driver slumped over the wheel. On closer inspection I could see that he was asleep (the after-effects of a drunken stupor). I was determined that he was not going to drive in that state so I found out where he lived, pushed him over to the passenger seat and drove his car to his house, closely followed by a colleague driving our CID car.

When this was done, we went back to the nick where a senior officer was waiting. He shouted at me, 'In my office. Where have you been?' I started to explain but he interrupted me and said, 'You've been off your patch and you've taken a man home who had been drinking. I know all this because he has rung me and told me.' I told him, 'I have run him home many times when he was drunk so I fail to see what the problem is.' He muttered something about insubordination and explained that the man was under surveillance on suspicion of buying and selling stolen cars and the officers were near to making an arrest when I showed up. They reported me to their Guvnor but the villain also reported me, hoping to get me into trouble.

This set my mind to thinking about a well-known story:

A non-conforming bird refused to fly south for the winter,
But the weather was now getting worse with snow,
So at last he took off and on getting to his required height
Ice formed on his wings.
Within a short time he fell into a farmyard, lying there unable to fly.
A cow passed by and crapped on the bird, who thought this was the end,
But the warmth of the manure warmed the bird and defrosted his wings.
Now being warm and happy, he started to sing.
Just then a cat came by and heard him singing,
Scraped away the manure and promptly ate the bird.

The moral of this story is:

Anyone who shits on you is not necessarily your enemy.
Anyone who gets you out of the shit is not necessarily your friend.
But if you are warm and happy in the shit – keep your bloody mouth shut.

Lesson learnt.

I went into a pub in Cricklewood for a meal with DC Mick Crofts when a few other members of the CID team came in. A man who looked like a copper saw us all together and bought us all a drink. I asked Mick who the man was but neither he nor any of the CID team knew him.

I went over to him and thanked him for the drink and then asked him which nick he was from. He replied, 'I've finished in the police now, the workload got me down.' I asked him his name and he replied, 'Dennis, Dennis Nilsen.' The time passed quickly and I made to leave when Nilsen asked which way I was going. I said that I was going down Cricklewood on my way home. He asked if I could give him a lift home as he lived near Cricklewood. I agreed and he got in my car. He directed me to his flat and as he got out he asked if I would like a nightcap, but I refused because I was keen to get home to my family. As it happened, these were probably the wisest words that I could have uttered since I had stood in a church many years before and said, 'I do.'

It wasn't long after my meeting with Nilsen that he was arrested for about fifteen murders of men whom he had enticed into his flat one way or another. His modus operandi was that once he got his victims into his flat he drugged them and then killed them. His flat in Cricklewood was full of the bodies of his victims before he moved to Muswell Hill, and he filled that flat, too.

He was caught when the drains became blocked. The unfortunate plumber, who was called in to see what was causing the blockage, discovered human remains. Nilsen was questioned and he stated that he had lost count of how many men he had killed.

I followed the trial with particular interest. He was found guilty and is now doing a recommended 25 years in prison. My feeling is that he should have been hanged for committing these offences.

Memories always come back whenever I get a blocked drain of how near I came to becoming a blockage in some drain or another. It certainly makes you think.

Lived to fight another day!

Night duty again and I was on patrol with Detective Constable Williams and Detective Constable Robinson. DC Williams was driving us along the Finchley Road when two cars loaded with people travelling in the same direction came swerving across the road. The drivers were acting like complete idiots. They stopped at the traffic lights so I jumped out and stopped one of the cars. I produced my warrant card and told the driver to pull over, which he did. The passenger then jumped out as I was telling the driver off for being stupid and punched me on the nose, so I arrested him for assaulting me. At the same time, I was trying frantically to stem the blood flowing from my nose. The man had a terrible temper and I expected another punch so in order to defend myself I pushed him into the police car.

He was taken to Finchley Police Station and charged. Afterwards he told me that he would have me hauled before my senior officers because he 'knew men in high places.' He added that he was confident the magistrate would then throw the case out and that he would get away with the charge.

The following morning he sat in Highgate Court as we waited for the case to be called, I asked him how he intended to plead and he replied, 'Not guilty, of course, this case has been sorted out at higher levels.'

The magistrate listened to my evidence without saying a word and at the end of the proceedings he dismissed the case, just as my assailant had predicted he would. I thought to myself, well it just goes to show how people in the right place *can* pull strings. Later, this man was to become one of the BBC's correspondents in the USA. It all fitted into place later when I remembered that a person with a criminal record cannot legally enter the USA. Some people can and do pull strings. I bet he does not assault police officers in the USA.

This case reminded me of a similar one some years earlier when I arrested four rich kids outside *The Pheasantry*, a high-class restaurant in the Kings Road, Chelsea. They had smashed the concrete pheasants that stood on the pillars outside the establishment.

They were taken to Chelsea Police Station where they were charged with causing criminal damage, which had been witnessed by four police officers. However, next day in Court their solicitor told the Magistrate that the four young men had just obtained their university degrees and had been celebrating. The Magistrate dismissed the case, saying it was a case of high jinks. When lads from council estates do the same thing they are referred to as yobs and are sentenced accordingly. What a system!

Late one evening I was sent with DCs Steve Bocking and Mick Crofts to Leytonstone to arrest a lad for burglary and serious assault. When we knocked at the door the suspect opened it. He straightaway realised who we were and tried to slam it shut. Steve put his foot in the door, pushed it open and in we went. We ran up the stairs and when we reached the top the suspect lashed out, hitting Steve full in the face. The lad was soon overpowered but still managed to give Steve another hard blow to the face before he went down. Steve was clearly hurt but he managed to handcuff the man who was still fighting mad. In fact, even in the police car on the way back to the nick he was still kicking out at us. We sent Steve off to the Divisional Surgeon for treatment. The suspect was charged and continued to fight like a mad man in the Station.

The following morning he still had not calmed down so he had to be handcuffed to me on one side and Mick Crofts on the other as we stood in the dock at Highgate Magistrates Court. Steve got in the witness box and asked the Magistrate to remand the prisoner in custody until the case could be heard at Crown Court because he was a danger to the public and he might abscond; furthermore, we needed to take his fingerprints. The Magistrate looked us up and down and then said, 'You've heard what the officer has said, so because of your acts of violence all three of you will go to prison and be remanded until your fingerprints are taken and then returned at a later date.' I started to say something but he stopped me with the threat of being in contempt of court. (I thought, that's it Jim, you are going down for a stretch in the nick but at least you'll get a rest.)

But there was to be no rest for me this time. The Clerk of the Court saved us by telling the Magistrate that the two men on the outside were police officers. The Magistrate apologised and told us that as we had all been handcuffed he thought we were all prisoners. Some people just don't listen do they? Silly old sod.

I'd been at Golders Green for sometime when I had to go to East Finchley where a murder had been committed at a Wedding Reception. I was told the complete story when I arrived at the scene and I then relayed it to my senior officer on his arrival.

It was during the wedding breakfast after all the presents had been laid out that matters took a turn for the worse. Most of the guests, including the bride's family and the groom's family, had got drunk and the two families decided to re-kindle a long-running feud. Because of all the booze they had consumed, they started to fight and it was not long before the room was a shambles of broken plates, food, and overturned tables.

Soon the bridegroom decided to join in the fighting and argued with one of the bride's uncles. Apparently this uncle had given the couple a carving set as a wedding present, little imagining that he would soon get it back. The groom suddenly picked up a carving knife and rammed it straight through his chest, killing him instantly.

The bridegroom was promptly handcuffed to two officers and taken away to the Station where he was charged with murder, which was later reduced to manslaughter because it had not been premeditated. He was sentenced to two years' imprisonment.

In my opinion, this was such a short sentence that it seemed to make a person's life appear cheap and worthless. It had taken us a long time to take statements from all the witnesses. They might as well have been run off on a photocopying machine as they nearly all said the same thing; nevertheless, the job had to be done.

On the second day we finally wrapped everything up. The boss man came back to take us for a drink (as they usually do after a murder enquiry is finished) and we all propped up the bar in our regular haunt, a Golders Green nightspot. Again, I was so tired that all I wanted to do was to go home but I knew it was still a case of: be it on your own head if you dare leave without permission.

As the evening wore on I saw my opportunity and lay on an unoccupied bench with cushions on it. (I've often been told that I can sleep on a clothesline.) Out of sight, I dozed off and all my troubles were soon forgotten.

I was jolted back to reality by a disturbance; I could hear swearing and shouting and as I jumped up I could see Bernie, the nightclub owner, in trousers and pyjama top, waving his arms and cursing. When I eventually came round, I heard him say, 'I locked up and went home at two o'clock when everyone had gone. I went to bed at five o'clock and then realised that I had locked you in the Club.' He lived five miles away and because he had driven back to let me out he was none too pleased with me. I said, 'Why didn't you leave me 'til morning?' He said, 'Not bloody likely with all this booze here.' I must admit that on that occasion booze was the last thing on my mind. But what a way to go.

Chapter Sixteen

BACK TO THE BURGLARY SQUAD

I was posted back to 'S' Division Burglary Squad for six months and the very first job we were assigned to, believe it or not, was a burglary!

We were in an area where burglary was prevalent and being night-time, as we cruised around in the car, we soon got our first call. 'Burglary in progress at 25 Rutland Road, the property of a police officer. See the informant, the police officer.' So off to Mill Hill we went. The officer was still in his pyjamas and standing at the gate when we arrived. He shouted out to us that the burglar had run out of the house and into the field at the back of the house. I jumped out of the car just as the two dog vans arrived and ran round the back of the house, across the garden, over the fence and into the field. I could see my quarry ahead and could easily have caught him when one of the dog handlers shouted, 'Stand still, we've let the two dogs go, they will go past you and catch him.' I did as they ordered and stood perfectly still; I knew what these animals were capable of on the command of their handler. The dogs sped past me (thank goodness) but they had only gone about fifty or sixty yards when they stopped.

What I saw next was extraordinary and not at all what I had expected. One dog jumped on the back of the other, enjoying what usually causes some embarrassment when it happens in the street. Not a suspect in sight, he had long gone, and all that was left was a dog and a bitch very much engaged and two very red-faced dog handlers. I was annoyed to put it mildly and told them to separate the dogs and go and catch the suspect.

However, our driver who was familiar with the area said he would drive round to the other side of the field and try to stop the suspect. He drove the car over the field and then got out of the car and waited. He did not have to wait very long before the man emerged and ran straight into his arms.

When the dog handlers eventually dared to show their faces back at the nick, they were ribbed rotten. Word soon got around and it wasn't long before we had let most of the 25,000 coppers in London know what had taken place that evening. But we had made our arrest, so it was not such a dog's breakfast after all.

One evening we were cruising around in the patrol car and I was in the back seat. The driver and my mate were busy in conversation as we passed the Orange Tree Public House in Totteridge Lane. This was, and still is, an area of great wealth. A lot of the houses, owned by the rich and famous, are extremely impressive.

Because of the rich pickings to be had, this was a favourite haunt for thieves and indeed in the preceding six months they had managed to steal a vast amount of cash and valuables. I was looking out for any opportunity to catch members of this fraternity when all of a sudden I saw an old rust bucket (an excuse for a car) with a couple of dodgy looking passengers inside. They drove into the entrance of one of the houses.

Meanwhile, my driver and the other officer were still deep in conversation and oblivious to what was happening. I tried a couple of times to intervene in their obviously rivetting discussion, but to no avail until I shouted 'Will you please shut up for a moment and pay attention to what is going on.' They immediately stopped gabbing and I told the driver to turn round and go back to the house. He did this and we entered the driveway of the house, just as the rust bucket had done a few minutes earlier.

The police driver turned off the car headlights and drove slowly. He stopped the car some distance from the house, we got out and walked slowly up to the house and saw that the front door had been smashed open. One officer went round to the back of the house and the other officer and I went in at the front door, or what was left of it. We proceeded to search the ground floor and on entering the lounge we saw a man sitting on the floor staring at us with his mouth wide open. I asked him if he lived there. He replied that he didn't. 'Do you own the place?' I asked. Again the answer was no. Then he said, 'Look, you know I've broken in here, isn't that enough for you lot?' He was unable to walk – having broken his ankle when he kicked the front door down – so we assisted him to the car and took him and his mate, who had been found at the rear of the property, to Whetstone Police Station.

Much later, he asked for seven other offences to be taken into consideration. Apparently his wife had thrown him out of the family home and he had nowhere to live so he had committed the burglaries so that he could be sent to prison where he would be given food and a bed.

His wish was duly granted.

This reminded me of a similar offence which occurred on another occasion. I was in a patrol car with the driver when a car passed and swerved in front of us. It was travelling at about sixty miles an hour in a thirty mile an hour area. We chased it up the Edgware Road and onto the A41. The driver was doing approximately ninety miles an hour when he swerved into the entrance of the M1. As he did so the car hit the kerb and headed directly for the central reservation, narrowly missing other vehicles. I radioed for assistance and gave a running commentary until Sierra Three took over the chase. We had also been joined by a car from the Hertfordshire Constabulary whose patch we were now on.

Way past Scratchwood's Service Area and we were still going; junction 11 of the M1 came and went, Luton vanished quickly into the distance behind us as we continued the chase. Suddenly, sparks flew from the bandit car as it hit another car, the impact taking the side off the runaway vehicle, but still it continued along the motorway, dragging jagged metal with it.

The driver of the car must then have panicked because he drove straight into the nearside embankment. As soon as the police cars had come to a stop, out jumped a dozen coppers who pulled the driver out so quickly that his feet didn't touch the ground. It was immediately obvious to all parties that he was drunk.

Evidently, he had had a row with his wife who had thrown him out of the house. I said to him, 'Just a row with your wife made you go on a drinking spree, drive like a lunatic, damage numerous vehicles, and endanger the lives of police and other people. You want locking up and the key throwing away.' He didn't show any remorse, which disgusted me, especially when I thought that his actions could have resulted in some fatalities.

By the time we got him to the Station I had calmed down. Just think, a small tiff with his wife (as happens to all of us from time to time) led to this incident. Good job we don't all take the same action or there would be no room in the police cells.

I found out later what the argument had been about. He had forgotten to pick his wife up from the hairdressers! It was obvious that she had forgiven him because before I left the nick she showed up and was taken to see him. When I went off duty I saw her crying on his shoulder, probably crying about the thousands that they might have to pay for all the damage her husband had caused.

A couple of weeks later we were called to Friern Barnet Mental Asylum where an alleged murder had been committed. But before we even got there, I couldn't believe my eyes when we drove by a woman up a tree in her front garden, some distance from the mental hospital. She had a tin of paint and was painting the whole tree, including the branches, the leaves, and the whole trunk. We looked over her fence and saw that she had also painted the house, the garden, the plants, the grass and the hedge – all in brilliant white paint! I thought to myself, 'I'm not hiring her to do my gardening, that's for sure.' And that was before we had even gone into the Asylum!

We soon forgot about her and concentrated instead on why we had been called to the Institution. We were told that one of the mental patients had punched another patient who had fallen and hit his head on a radiator and died. The law views this as an unlawful killing, so we had to go through the motions of charging him, knowing that he could never be convicted because he was mentally unsound at the time of the incident.

When I attended the post mortem the doctor showed me part of the dead man's lungs and told me that he had died of bronchitis and pneumonia. The case was never brought to court because the cause of death was pneumonia, not murder. It saved the country a substantial amount of money, time and manpower, but I could have certainly murdered a pint and a ciggy that day after seeing the state of that guy's lungs.

I had just entered the office one morning and before I had a chance to have my first cuppa of the day the telephone started ringing. I answered it and on the other end of the line was a Manchester Police officer who told me that a lorry laden with stolen goods was on its way to Scratchwood's service area on the M1. This lorry had been stopped the previous night by Manchester Police and all the thieves had been arrested, but the officers were not entirely satisfied so they negotiated with the driver who agreed to continue his journey to London. Their goal was to find out who was involved in the scam at the London-end of things and to make arrests there as well, thereby capturing the whole gang. An undercover Manchester police officer had been assigned to travel with the driver in the cab of the lorry, which was well on its way to Scratchwood, so we did not have much time to get ourselves organised to help our colleagues. The operation swung into operation under the command of a Detective Sergeant.

A running commentary was kept up by the police officers who had been assigned to keep a lookout for the vehicle on the M1. They gave us a continuous summary of the progress of the lorry until it eventually turned into Scratchwood. The other gang members were waiting there to transfer the illegal loot onto their vehicles. They were quickly surrounded, arrested and charged with handling stolen goods and then locked up, awaiting trial. When the day of the trial came we were all well prepared and ready to go, but the case didn't even get off the ground before the Judge dismissed it and threw it out, leaving some very shocked police officers.

The reason the Judge gave for his decision was that the contents of the lorry were no longer stolen goods because they had been in police possession. Furthermore, due to the presence of the police officer in the cab of the lorry, the Judge regarded it as entrapment.

The villains all lived happily ever after and they laughed at us as they left the courtroom. It was certainly felt by all the officers present that day that the law is an ass.

I came on late turn duty one evening and was told that most of the team were raiding a house on an estate. I was asked to assist.

Off I went, armed with a pair of handcuffs and when I arrived at the scene I was told to wait outside. Once the prisoners had been passed over to me, I was to handcuff them to the fence. (I must mention here that at that time handcuffs were issued by the Station Officer, minus the keys, and only he could release a prisoner who had been handcuffed.) So I waited.

As I waited, I played about with the handcuffs, spinning them around. I fixed one end to my wrist and continued to spin them. All of a sudden, bang! the other end made contact with the fence (Lord knows how) and yes, you've guessed it, I was locked good and proper on to the fence. I didn't worry because I knew I could slide my knife down the side and release the ratchet. I had done it many times when fellow officers had played tricks on me in the past.

I put my hand in my pocket – no knife. I tried my other pockets but to no avail, my knife was definitely not there. Then I remembered I had changed my suit that morning and forgotten to transfer my knife. Well, was I for it if the Guvnor showed up. I knew he would teach me a lesson and leave me there.

The situation called for some drastic action. First of all I tried to knock on the front door of the property where I was waiting, but I could not reach it. Then it occurred to me that I could reach it with my feet, so I kicked the door. A dear old lady answered and I asked her if she had a thin bladed knife. I explained why I needed it but it was obvious that she thought I was a villain. I showed her my warrant card and explained what a daft thing I had done. She eventually gave me the benefit of the doubt and gave me a knife as I had asked. I slid the blade down by my wrist, the ratchet thankfully gave way and I was free. Just in time, because the first prisoner was coming out of the door. I gave the knife back to the lady who had saved my skin and locked the prisoner into the place I had unintentionally been keeping warm for him. The Guvnor came out with the key some time later, released the prisoner, and we took him to the nick.

It wasn't long before word of my little escapade got around the Station. Evidently, the Beat Officer knew the little old lady and she had spilled the beans. But at least I'm free now.

We were called to burglar alarms during the day and during the night as well. There was one alarm that went off most evenings of the week and officers attended every time as quickly as they could. The owner of the premises was a well-known businessman at the time and his firm manufactured cigarette lighters.

It wasn't long before I twigged his little scam. He had numerous gambling friends in for dinner most nights and after they had finished their meal they would lay huge bets on the table about how long it would take police to respond to the alarm being set off. The winner took all for the nearest guess as to how long it took.

We decided not to say anything and simply waited for the next time we were called to turn off the alarm. When it came, everyone was advised about the gentleman's scam and so we all waited, and waited, and waited, until an hour went by before we responded.

When we eventually arrived at the scene, the owner was absolutely furious because he had lost his bet. He complained bitterly to me, so I came straight back at him with 'Do you think the police have got nothing better to do than come running to you every time you set off the alarm on purpose?' – and left.

The amusing finale to this story was that a few months later the alarm went off, this time for real, and we didn't hurry to the scene, thinking it was another scam. But this time it was for real and the premises were burgled. That taught him to cry wolf.

I had spent two wonderful years at Golders Green Police Station but now it was time to move on. I was sent to Borehamwood, which was the north-ernmost Police Station of the Metropolitan Police District.

There were quite a few factories out that way and there was also Elstree Film Studios. I was worried that things might seem a little quieter than I was used to but soon after I arrived there I found it every bit as busy as other Stations where I had served.

Still on 'S' Division Burglary Squad, I saw a man race past me with two coppers on his tail. I thought it best to join the chase and off I sped and quickly overtook my colleagues. I saw the man climb up a drainpipe and onto the flat roof of a shop. He then ran across the shop roof and jumped down the other side.

I climbed up the drainpipe after him and across the roof. I then followed him down the other side, close on his heels. He ran up a railway embankment, up and over a 12-foot high fence and down the other side. I did the same and landed on railway property at the same time as he did. 'Alright, I give up,' he panted. I grabbed him and made him climb back over the fence and into the arms of the waiting policemen.

Later I asked them what the suspect had done. One replied, 'I don't know, when he saw us he ran, so we ran after him.' I shook in my boots, I had just deprived a man of his liberty and they had no idea what the man had done! I then saw the pound signs cross my eyes of the compensation payout for a wrongful arrest and I was sure that it would not be long before this guy had worked this out for himself.

The man looked at his watch and said, 'Oh, I must go,' but I then thought of a get-out clause. I told him I was arresting him and proceeded to caution him. The other officers took me on one side and asked me why I was cautioning him. I replied, 'I know, and he knows.' I turned to the suspect and said, 'Take off that watch.' He did as he was told and I looked at it. It was a solid gold Bucher Gerard specially-made watch, worth about £2,000, which was clearly more than most ordinary people could afford. I had only seen these watches on one occasion and that was when I had visited the factory in Watford.

Off to the nick we went, where I was greeted as the sprinter of the day. The story had gone around the nick that I, a 45-year old man, had outrun the prisoner who was only 23 years old. The other two officers were both 20-year-olds. Well, the old man was certainly not such a mature officer now.

Enquiries were made about the watch and it was found to be one of a few that had been stolen. We soon found out that a jeweller in Wembley had the other stolen watches. His shop was raided and he was arrested. In the fullness of time convictions were obtained. They certainly had to watch their step in the future!

We obtained information that stolen bottles of Chanel No.5 perfume could be found at Elstree Film Studios. Enquiries were made and the information was found to be correct, so we took out search warrants for the homes of the vendors where the property was allegedly being kept.

It was a nice morning as we set off at 4am (some would say this was still the middle of the night and I think I would agree with them) for Tower Hamlets. We arrived at the first suspect's house and banged on the door. He opened it and shook with fear when he found out who we were. In we went; we certainly didn't wait for an invitation. It was my turn to shake when I saw that he had a big dog guarding the door to the living room. We ordered the suspect to remove the dog and began our search. Well, you can imagine our surprise when we opened the door of one of the bedrooms, because stacked from floor to ceiling were cases and cases of Chanel No.5. In fact, we found not just one room like this but four. The booty was in every conceivable place you could imagine. There was enough perfume to last 500 women 500 years. We needed vans to transfer the bottles of perfume to the nick and a gang of stevedores to move them. The rest of the day was written off just shifting the stuff from his house.

After many hours we finished and feeling very tired and hungry we went to a nearby café for a meal. As we walked in, the occupants of the café sniffed the air and started to leave because the scent was overpowering. We must have smelled like the inside of the Grasse perfume factory. It took days to get rid of the smell.

Other houses were raided and more perfume was found. The vendors were taken away and placed in police custody. The thieves received prison sentences and the handlers were fined heavily. Later, the property was returned to its rightful owner, but as someone pointed out, 'this case smells.'

Our day of fame arrived at last when we were approached by ITV to make a documentary about burglary and the Burglary Squad. This involved Camera! Sound! Action! every minute of the day, and sometimes during the night as well.

The film crew followed us with cameras when we were in the cars, at raids, on chases, recovering stolen property – absolutely everywhere we went.

On one particular day we were keeping observation on a house. As usual, the cameras were watching us watching the villains, but on this occasion they blew out (ruined) our operation and it had to be called off very quickly.

The only other times I appeared on the small screen was when I helped in the making of *Modesty Blaize* and in a shoe advertisement for Hush Puppies. But this sort of thing wasn't what policing was about and we were glad when eventually they left us in peace.

When the documentary *Burglary Squad* was eventually shown on television, the crew had made it look very interesting. But I certainly was not Hollywood-bound after my performance, so Clint Eastwood didn't have to worry too much.

It was my day off: so I found it hard to understand why some idiot decided to spoil it all by thoughtlessly killing another fellow human being. I was happily lazing in bed on a lovely Sunday morning, thinking that I wasn't going to shave that day and that I would lounge around until my lunch was on the table, then continue lounging around all afternoon reading the Sunday newspaper and watching a classic black and white film on television.

But just as I was dozing off to sleep the telephone rang, disturbing my slumber. I guessed who it was so I hid my head under the covers, but not for long because my wife shouted, 'You're wanted at Whetstone Police Station right away, they've had a murder during the night.' I reluctantly jumped out of bed and before I knew it I was driving down Totteridge Lane towards the nick. My thoughts turned to the murder. There had been 47 murders in the previous twelve months on 'S' Division alone, and in addition to our Division there were another 21 Divisions in the Metropolitan Police area. The incidence of murders had certainly increased in the previous year. There was never this number of killings when we had the death penalty.

The last murder we had been called to involved an Indian woman who had two children. Her husband had died and she had a new partner, but sadly he did not want her children and she had killed them. A WDC dealt with the murders by herself because the powers that be did not consider that the murders warranted the employment of a team of detectives.

I soon arrived at Whetstone where I learned that a disco had been held the previous night at a local pub and fighting had broken out between the rival suitors of a young lady. The fight ended when somebody was stabbed and died later in hospital. All we had to go on at the time was the statements of three witnesses, so Detective Sergeant Havard and I went to the first witness's address. The other two witnesses were also present, so we separated them before questioning them further. Once they had all been questioned, we returned to the nick.

Sergeant Havard and I went to lunch and naturally we discussed the case. We both came to the conclusion that there was something that the three witnesses had not told us so we decided to go and see them again that afternoon. As we drove up to the house, we could see all three talking in the garage. However, when we approached them they clammed up. Silence ruled. I told them that they were suspects and we were taking them to the nick for further enquiries. This shook them and they soon gave us the name and address of the murderer and made statements to this effect.

We went to the alleged murderer's home and his mother opened the door. She said, 'Yes, I know why you are here, come in.' Her son was sitting on the settee. One thing that struck me as I entered the room was that you wouldn't have given him a second glance because he just appeared to be a frightened young man. In fact, I have found that most murderers do not look how you expect them to look. Nonetheless, he was arrested and taken to the nick. He readily admitted committing the offence. We searched him and then he was detained until the Detective Chief Superintendent arrived to charge him.

At 8pm he was charged and all the loose ends were tied up. We went off to the pub where the Chief Superintendent bought us all a pint before we made our way home to await the next bout of crimes. Still no day off.

We were travelling along West Hendon Broadway on our way to the Police Station when a man ran out of a doorway screaming in agony. As he reached the centre of the road we saw that his skin was falling off his body, and then he fell to the ground.

Apparently he and his family owned the local fish and chip shop. They had finished the morning fry and the husband and son went up to the flat above to have a rest. The son went back to his bed and the father fell asleep on the settee, leaving the wife to clean up the shop ready for the evening trade. Evidently she had got very annoyed at having to do this chore so she re-lit the burners, boiled the oil, grabbed a bucket and filled it with the hot oil, then went upstairs to the living room and threw the contents of the bucket all over her husband. In desperation, and in great agony, he ran out into the street – which was where we came in.

We called for an ambulance and the husband was taken to hospital in a matter of minutes. Meanwhile, we went into the house to make some enquiries. On arrival we found that the wife had done the same thing to her son and he was in a terrible state as well. We again called for an ambulance and I accompanied him to the hospital hoping to get a statement – or at worse a dying declaration – from either him or his father.

As the night wore on, the two victims remained unconscious in adjoining rooms whilst the nurses and doctors did what they could for them. Sadly, they never recovered and they both died early the next morning. I went home to have a shower and a meal and then returned to the Station to write up what I knew so far before making further enquiries.

The wife was held in custody at Holloway Womens' Prison until her trial and she was given two life sentences for her crimes. Who would want a mother like her?

The Chief Superintendent's driver took some time off, so I had to drive the Guvnor for a day or two. We received a call to go to the home of Mr MacWhirter of the *Guinness Book of Records* fame. We were at Barnet Police Station when we received the call so we were able to get to the address in five or six minutes.

Mr MacWhirter had never done anything in his life to deserve a death threat. The IRA hoped to use him as a tool to put pressure on the Government to re-unite Ireland. When we got to the scene, there was not much left, only a mass of tangled metal where this poor man had been blown up with a bomb specially made for the purpose. We left the scene quickly, as we were not involved with the investigation. Will we ever understand why murders like this are committed?

We were called one afternoon to a murder that had been committed in Cricklewood. We smashed our way in and found a young girl had been stabbed. We had got to the scene so quickly that we were able to apprehend the suspected murderer.

Enquiries later revealed that the young lady (I won't name her) and her husband had lived near Hyde Park. They had visited their local pub one evening and got talking to a young, homeless man and, feeling sorry for him, they invited him back to their house to stay until he found a flat of his own. He enjoyed this arrangement immensely and so he stayed for six months. During this time, the wife started having feelings for the lodger and it wasn't long before he started having mutual feelings for her. They eventually became lovers and were so close that they could not be parted.

In the meantime, the husband was being brushed aside until they finally pushed him out of the house. He kept returning in the hope that he could be reconciled with his wife but there was no room for him and he felt like an outsider in his own home. The situation became so unbearable that the wife and the lodger moved to a flat in Cricklewood. The wife got a typing job at a local firm and it was in the building where the company was situated that she met her end.

Her husband continued to want her back but he did not know where she had gone. He was beside himself thinking of the two lovers together and whenever he went out looking for her he took a knife. Eventually, he found her at her place of work. He entered the office, pulled out the knife and chased her out of the office. She ran into the toilet and locked the door behind her. He kicked down the door and stabbed her, 17 times. She probably died on either the first or second stabbing, but in his frenzy he could not stop stabbing her.

Although this was clearly a crime of passion, the circumstances were such that a charge of murder was laid against him. This was because he had looked for his wife with intent to hurt her with the knife. However, the Judge decided before the trial that the charge should be reduced to manslaughter and he would not allow the evidence about the man carrying the knife to be presented to the jury. As a result of the Judge's instructions, the husband was given a two-year prison sentence. So another one got away.

Taffy Cornwall joined us on the Burglary Squad at Boreham Wood. He was married to a Scotswoman and they lived in flat in Burnt Oak. On one particular day, Taffy was keeping observation on a suspect and he was a long way from the CID office. Complete radio silence had to be maintained on this occasion. During the morning, his wife rang me and asked to speak to her husband. On learning that he could not be contacted, she told me that the roof of their flat had fallen in. I told her that I would try and get a message to Taffy.

As time passed, his wife rang me again with the same story, but he still could not be contacted. This went on in the same way for the rest of the morning.

During the afternoon she rang again and told me that the rain was now coming in through the roof and that she was going to her friend who lived in Stanmore. She also told me that she had advised the landlord that she was going. Shortly afterwards, Taffy rang in and I told him that he was wanted urgently and he said that he would get back to the office as soon as he could.

It was dark by the time he returned to the Station. He told me that he had made an arrest and had to do the paperwork. I told him that his wife had been trying to contact him all day and told him about the roof having fallen in. He then asked me what she had said, to which I replied 'It's a braw bricht moonlicht nicht ternicht, d'ye ken.' Everyone in the office collapsed in hysterics.

Taffy had already reported the condition of the roof to the landlord and was waiting to be moved. I took him to where his wife was staying that evening and they all appreciated my joke.

A security van robbery had occurred at Elstree Airport and we were making enquiries in the area. We entered the Airport, made enquiries at the hangers, the offices and anywhere we thought people might be able to help. We knew that the money had been taken away by air, or should I say we had a good idea it had been. We were made welcome in the offices and a nice pot of tea was made for us. As we were drinking our tea, a pilot asked us if we would like a trip in his aeroplane, which we accepted.

Three of us climbed into his Piper Commanche and he took off. We flew over the section where we worked and when I looked down I couldn't believe my eyes: I saw two men loading gear from a house into a van. I asked the pilot to go around again until we were low enough to be able to read the registration number of the vehicle.

As soon as we landed, we raced to the house and arrested the two men whom we had spotted from the air. One of them asked, 'How did you know we were here? There were no neighbours living nearby and we couldn't be seen from the road.' I replied, 'What about the aeroplane that just flew over you, didn't you notice it? We were on board and that's how we spotted you.' 'Bloody hell,' he said, 'you've even got planes now, you lot think of everything.'

Our luck was in that day until the Guvnor asked where we had been. When he heard about the arrests he congratulated us on a good piece of work. Good job he didn't know we had been up in an aeroplane!

One of the lads who knew the whole story said, 'If you fell into a bucket of shit, you'd come out smelling of roses.'

Another break-in occurred some weeks later in Burnt Oak. When we arrived at the scene the suspect was still on the premises and so we went all round the property, checking all the exits. We found that they were locked, possibly from the inside. Officers were then posted at vantage points so that the suspect had no escape route.

We acquired a sledgehammer to break down the front door and my colleagues volunteered me for this job. Well, I took one almighty swipe at the door with all my strength… and missed. However, the force of my swing and the weight of the hammer made me spin around and I managed to make contact on the second time round. There was a short pause when nothing happened and then suddenly the door gave way and flew open. I fell inside and thought that I had better drop the hammer just in case I carried on through the house and out the other side.

I looked around downstairs and could see nothing so I came back to the foot of the stairs. As I looked up in the half-light there, I saw a lad standing and staring at me. He drew a long knife from a sheath in his trousers and told me to go no further. Without any warning, he dived towards me with the sword aimed in my direction. I managed to dodge to one side and stuck one foot out. He tripped over it and landed on the floor. As he did so, he tried to lash out at me and I quickly stood on the weapon. We handcuffed him and his knife was thrown out of the way. He was taken away in the van to West Hendon nick.

He was later returned to a local mental hospital but he would have been the death of me if I had not reacted so quickly. Lady Luck was certainly with me that day.

I was on duty with Ken Graham when we saw a quantity of booze being taken into a house in Hendon at Five Ways Corner. We obtained a search warrant and went to the premises to take a look.

After knocking at the door, we quickly entered, showing the warrant to the occupier. We went into action, inspecting the premises for contraband. Well, we didn't have to search far for the booze: it was stacked high in the lounge and in the dining room. There was every type of booze you could possibly think of and more besides. The owner's wife then came into the lounge and said, 'I'm so glad you have come to collect this liquor, I just can't stand seeing it cluttering up my rooms any longer. Just pay your money and then get this lot out of here.' She had obviously mistaken us for customers who had come to purchase some of this 'duty free' booze. When we explained to her who we were, she was, to put it mildly, a little upset.

We asked the occupier where the booze had come from and he replied 'I've fetched it from Alconbury US Air Force PX Stores. I've bought it and paid for it, it's for my mates.' We advised him that it was illegal to buy and sell this booze. He was charged under Custom and Excise regulations. However, he had no previous convictions so he was only fined a nominal sum. The booze was confiscated by Customs and Excise to be taken away and destroyed (honest, Guvnor!)

Oh, by the way, the Right Honourable John Smith, the former leader of the Labour Party and now deceased, represented the man at court.

Customs officers had been keeping observation on a particular house for some time after following some suspects from the docks at Dover. Having collected the necessary evidence by way of photographs and by filming the suspects, the officers were ready to raid the premises. I've done quite few raids with the customs officers and, let me put it this way, their reckless attitude can't have won them many friends. They certainly don't show any great diplomatic skills when they carry out their raids.

On this occasion they came to us and asked for assistance. Along we went with them to an address in Mill Hill. The customs officers don't bother knocking on doors, they just kick the doors in back and front. They then usually carry out a search. Anything they have looked at and which is not taken away as evidence is just discarded.

On this particular morning, their method of working was no different. They had crowbars and lifted up the floor. No stone was left unturned, stairs were taken apart, lofts thoroughly searched, and they even took the bathroom apart. Well, they got a good result due to the thoroughness of their search and came up with thousands of pounds worth of drugs.

Later that day we again helped them to search a number of other premises and again they displayed their painstaking attention to detail and came up with more goodies.

All the suspects were arrested and a taken into custody at West Hendon Police Station. At their subsequent trial they all received long sentences.

No applications for compensation were sent to Customs and Excise for the damage done to the properties. Not that much would have come from such a claim because customs are not liable for damage caused to the places they raid. In fact, the criminals had rented some of the places that were raided on this occasion, so the landlord had to pick up the bill. I sometimes feel that the Government backs Customs and Excise to the hilt. Not like the police force.

We had just returned to Golders Green after dealing with a burglary when we were called to a party on Hampstead Hill. It was late at night by the time we arrived and walked in to discover that a big fight was in progress. Fists were flying, weapons were being used and injured people were everywhere.

I dealt with a woman who had had a glass smashed into her face. The glass had cut a complete circular gash around her nose and mouth and some of the glass was still sticking out of the wound. I recognised her as our canteen manager. She had been attending the party with her husband.

Being held at the side of the room was the man who had attacked her. Apparently the woman's husband had been in the kitchen talking to the attacker (who was homosexual) while she was dancing in the front room. When she went into the kitchen she grabbed her husband to encourage him to dance with her. Without a moment's hesitation, the other man struck her with his glass, breaking it into her face. He had been propositioning the husband and he had not been best pleased to be interrupted by the woman.

The attacker was charged with causing Grievous Bodily Harm and in due course was sent to prison. The lady never got over the attack. She never worked again and apparently became very withdrawn, hiding herself away as much as she could.

Chapter Seventeen

DREAMING OF WALKING AGAIN

Meanwhile, I was still in hospital and dreaming of the day when I would be able to walk again. My physiotherapist, Mrs Israel, worked on me night and day until I could take twenty steps unaided, but unfortunately the stitches in my back had to remain in place as an infection in the wound was getting worse. In fact, the whole hospital was infected and no one knew how to combat the germ which was causing the problem.

Then came the day I was told I would have to be moved to another hospital as things were getting out of hand, the bug was rampant. I was sent to the Police Hospital at Hendon and stayed there for 21 days.

At last the day arrived when my stitches were to be removed. The doctor decided to take every other stitch out on the first day and the remainder would be removed the next day. My physiotherapy continued until I collapsed again, paralysed from the waist down, and I was taken back to Portland Street hospital immediately.

I lay in hospital for several more months with no one knowing what to do next. Numerous tests were carried out, including x-rays, and I received more therapy, but to no avail. I'd now been continuously in four hospitals over a period of two and a half years.

One day, a Mr Jones, a Surgeon, came to see me. He told me that the broken bones had moved again and were pressing on the spine but I would have to wait until they had moved away from the spinal cord before they could be operated on.

Thankfully, after another four or five months, feeling returned to my right leg and to the lower half of my body. The surgeon told me that he would take a chance and operate on me again – but I would have to wait as he had a long waiting list.

Once again I had plenty of time to reflect on days gone by and a smile crossed my face as I remembered the following incident.

I was called into the front office at Golders Green Police Station and told to see a young lady and her boyfriend who were in the interview room. When I introduced myself the young lady, who was a BBC television producer, told me all about her job and as we talked I told her all about the stories I had recorded over the years. She tried to persuade me to go on television, but I declined.

I asked her why she had come to the Station. She told me that she had seen a newspaper advertisement offering a house for rent in Golders Green. As she and her fiancé were due to marry shortly they thought they would go and view the house so they telephoned the number given and arranged to view the property. When they arrived at the address they were told to wait in a room for their turn to view the property. There were eight other couples already waiting in the room for the same purpose.

When their turn came, they were ushered into a room by a man who interviewed them before showing them round the house. They were quite happy with what they saw and told him so. He demanded a £300 deposit, in cash. The fiancé went to a nearby bank to get the money and gave it to the man. The house was then theirs to rent. However, as they were leaving the house, another couple came in. This couple told them that they too had paid a deposit on the house and added that they had just met another couple who had also paid £300 to the owner.

On hearing this, both couples went back inside and demanded that their money be returned to them there and then. The owner flew into a raging temper and refused. He became quite violent and threw all the would-be tenants out of the house.

I took a written statement from the couple. With Detective Constable Williams, I went to the address that had been advertised and which had attracted so many clients. We entered the building and saw still more prospective tenants waiting! It was clear that the scam was still continuing. DC Williams and I made our way to the room where the clients were being interviewed. The owner immediately jumped up and told us to wait our turn. We thrust our warrant cards under his nose and told the other people to wait outside.

I asked the man if he was the owner of the property. To my astonishment he said, 'No, the owner is in Africa and he has asked me to rent the property out for him whilst he is away.' We continued probing until he told us the truth. The owner had only asked him to look after the property whilst he was away. The man then went on to admit the offence of theft of the deposits.

After he was arrested, we found a bag of cash totalling £2,640. He admitted that his takings the previous day had been very good and that he had collected over £7000. However, he had spent some of the money the same night.

We cautioned him that it was unlawful to take a deposit for rent of a property and that all the money would have to be returned to the rightful owners.

He went to court and was found guilty on three counts. He was given a short term in prison and had to pay a heavy fine.

Following this, would you believe it, my two original witnesses once again tried to get me to the studios to tell my tales, and again I refused.

There are a lot of gullible people in this world but there are always greedy vultures ready to relieve people of their wealth and then disappear with the spoils. Greed being the word.

We received information that drugs were being sold to kids at the gates of a school in Boreham Wood and so we decided to mount an observation. We had no success at all for over a week so we decided to ask some of the students if they could help. Fortunately, one lad gave us the lead we desperately needed. He gave us the address of the people who were selling the drugs and also told us where he had seen drugs being collected.

Our next move was to keep a watch on the premises whilst one of our officers obtained a search warrant. He returned after a short while, armed with the warrant. When we approached the door a woman was also waiting to be let in and as soon as she was admitted we followed her in. After the warrant was shown to the occupier we saw on a table all the usual accessories associated with drugs – a set of weighing scales, a scoop, plastic bags, and a small bag containing white powder. We also found a considerable amount of money on an adjacent table together with a bankbook showing a credit balance of £800. The occupants admitted selling and possessing drugs and allowing the premises to be used for these offences. They were taken to the nick and charged.

Later, when they appeared in court, they were granted legal aid with the assistance of their solicitor. As all the money they had accrued through their illegal dealing in drugs had been stashed away or spent, instead of being deposited in bank accounts, they were able to plead poverty and therefore were able eligible for legal aid. They had managed to acquire this solicitor at short notice and received advice from him to plead not guilty and to go for trial. If they had decided not to go for trial, the maximum sentence they could have been given by a Magistrate was six months' imprisonment with only a £200 maximum fine. However, the solicitor was keen to go to trial (not for the good of his clients but to line his own pocket) and in consequence, on being found guilty, they were fined £2000 and sent to prison for two years. As a result of bad advice, they ended up having their possessions confiscated, their child was put in care, and their mortgaged house was repossessed. I rest my case.

The wedding anniversary – I know every husband loves this day immensely. In fact, he loves it so much that he usually forgets it. I'm sure most men remember two weeks before, or one week before, or even two days before, but completely forget when the day arrives. I have been no exception – on a number of occasions.

I was at work early one morning when I sat at my desk and turned over the page of the calendar and saw the date. I saw it was 5th March, my wedding anniversary. What an idiot I was to forget it *again* , so in a panic I rushed out of the office and bought a card. But I didn't know what to do next. Then someone came up with a good idea – why not reserve a surprise table for two at the French restaurant in East Finchley? Great idea, I thought, so I rang the restaurant and then went home and left the anniversary card on the dining room table.

I rang my wife at work and told her that I had a surprise for her and to be ready to be picked up at 6.30pm. By the time she returned from work

I had showered and changed and away we went to this delightful restaurant in East Finchley. The table was lit with candles and it was very romantic. We sat down and I was so proud and pleased with myself that I hadn't forgotten that this day was our anniversary. (Alright, it might have slipped my mind just momentarily earlier in the day.)

The waiters hovered over us, one stood at the rear door and the manager stood close by. We had a drink while studying the menu, the first course was delivered, enjoyed, and cleared away. Then, over a bottle of wine, I said to my wife, 'Do you suspect that something is wrong here?' She is very intuitive and replied, 'Yes, that man is guarding the back door and those two waiters have never left or taken their eyes off us.' We had an extremely uneasy feeling and did not find it easy to relax. The manager then left his post at the rear but continued to watch us. The two waiters were still guarding us, stationed beside our table.

I'd had enough by this stage and called the manager over to ask him what on earth was going on. He then told me that the police had telephoned him that afternoon to warn him that a man and a woman named Beard, who were both wanted criminals, had been spotted in the area. The officer then added that one of their favourite tricks was to eat in expensive restaurants and then run out without paying the bill. They were wanted all over London and the police had told him to ring the Station as soon as possible if he spotted them. This he had done.

The manager said that if I paid my bill there and then, he would let us go out through the rear exit without any fuss before the police got to the restaurant, to avoid upsetting the other customers. I looked up and who should I see but my colleague Steve Bocking peering through the front window of the restaurant, so I said to the manager, 'It's too bloody late, they're here,' and to his amazement I laughed. I could see the panic on his face, thinking about his other customers, so I relieved his feelings and showed him my warrant card. When he realised that I was a police officer he could see the funny side of the prank. He went over to Bocking and the other officers who had been involved and invited this load of comedians into the restaurant to help us celebrate a grand occasion. A great time was had by one and all; even the other customers joined in our anniversary celebration. What a brilliant ending to a day that had started so badly. (But don't tell my wife that I forgot, will you!)

In the police world, humour and what you might call childish behaviour and pranks provide a lifeline to police officers. You've often heard the saying, 'laugh or you will cry' and this was certainly true in the Job. It is better to see the funny side of a situation otherwise you will crack up or turn to drink as a way of coping with very sad events. I attended a post mortem of a young lad and during the examination we cracked jokes, but at the same time our eyes filled with tears at the thought that this was someone's child or grandchild. We were never as hard as we pretended to be.

I've tried to be even and fair all my life and I've treated villains and victims with equal respect. Except for violence: I was always hard on villains who used violence in any crime. People such as the Moors murderers, in my opinion, should have been topped together with all those guilty of stabbings, shootings and murders.

Going on with this, I think youngsters should be taught a short sharp lesson at an early age. They should know the difference between right and wrong before they progress to theft, violence and even murder. It never harmed us in our days.

Crime starts in the home, so it should be checked in the home. Parents who tolerate small misdeeds by children will find that they develop from there, and before long those same children will move up to crimes outside the home. More leads to more, when they know they can get away with it, and at 17 years old, they are fully fledged criminals.

One case that springs to mind is that of the off-duty police officer who was travelling with his wife and family on a train when they were threatened by a youth. When the police officer's level of tolerance ran out he whacked the youth and the repercussions were such that he nearly lost his job. If it had been me and he had threatened my family, I would certainly have lost my job because they would have had to pick the lout up off the rail tracks.

As we lose police officers from our streets, the time is fast approaching when vigilante rules and vigilante punishment will follow. I believe the present government is to blame for this current lack of control.

Vicious criminals get away in courts with crime; judges either give light sentences or throw cases out, because they think the police are unfair. All governments say, 'We are going to get tough on criminals.' When, we hear you cry, when? They have got tough on police officers, prison officers and the like, but when are they really going to get tough on criminals?

One thing I can say is that my own two boys have turned out well in life. But most of this is down to my wife. One is now 44 and the other 41. My oldest son is a travel manager for one of the largest banks in Europe and the other is an accountant. They both now have families of their own to bring up.

Thank you for letting me have my say for a few minutes, and now back to the Burglary Squad!

The drugs problem flared up again in the Burnt Oak area. Observations were being carried out in a variety of places. We found needles in alleys and remains of containers that had held drugs, but we couldn't get a lead on where the stuff was coming from – until we got our first arrest in the area. A man was caught in possession of a cigarette containing 'grass', and after a lot of questioning he eventually told us where and how he got the cigarette. Four of us, including Mick Jones who was our driver, went to the address we had been given, a public house in the Edgware Road in Burnt Oak. We entered the pub on a Friday night and it was packed with customers. We approached the landlord, who was pulling pints, and asked if we could talk to him in private. 'Come back tomorrow, I'm busy,' he replied.

We were not happy with his unhelpful attitude so Mick shouted, 'This pub is closed until further notice, please leave now.' The landlord immediately stopped what he was doing and stared at us in amazement.

The Duty Inspector was sent for and he backed Mick's action. The pub was cleared and stayed closed all weekend. Some of the customers were searched on their way out and were arrested for drug offences and by the time we had carried out a search of the pub we had managed to fill a large carrier bag full of drugs. Most of it was found on the floor where it had been dropped.

We were pleased to have put a stop to the drug activity at this pub but of course the drug users and their suppliers moved on to another venue. A losing battle.

I hate writing about the following incident because it disturbed me very much when it happened. In fact, even 25 years on it still upsets me. I lost heart the night I returned to Boreham Wood and saw some of my fellow officers being dishonest. Crime was something I had been fighting throughout my police service. These men were people I had looked up to for guidance and help in maintaining obedience to the law.

One evening I drove into the Station yard and saw some police officers loading office furniture into the CID observation van. It included a desk, a chair, a filing cabinet and other items. An officer I knew very well was standing nearby and I asked him what was going on. He replied, 'It's none of your business.' I was furious and said, 'Well, I'm going to make it my business.' He thought about it for a moment and then told me the whole story.

A senior officer's son was starting up a business and he needed office furniture, so he ordered his police officers to take the furniture out of the nick and deliver it to his son's address. The others were told to keep it a secret from me (he didn't like me because I was one of the few officers who wouldn't regularly put a bottle of whisky on his desk). The new furniture had been ordered and delivered to the Station but it was then deleted from the Station's inventory and somehow or the other it was 'written off'.

When the senior officer found out that I knew about his little scam, he could not face me. He got someone to post me to Whetstone out of harm's way. But I knew from that day that he was no better than the common criminals I arrested. He was, in other words, a thief.

Chapter Eighteen

MOUNTAINS TO CLIMB

During my police service, I worked with some good men. When we had some spare time we did charity work for the under-privileged, the crippled, the orphans and many other needy people. We raised thousands and thousands of pounds each year to make their lives a little better and to give them some little luxury that they were missing out on. Even though it was something small, it made someone happy, and as someone once wrote: 'One man can't change the world, but together we can change the world for one man.'

Every winter we put on a Christmas pantomime. Our first job was to scrounge enough presents for these underprivileged children. Off we went to Bang & Olufson where we managed to obtain some records. Then we called on local jewellers, fruiterers, sweet shops, in fact any shop or any company that could give us something for the kids. Then we scrounged scene sets and paint; in fact all of the sets on stage were scrounged. When this was done, we went to Elstree Studios and scrounged all the lights, grease paint, make up and machinery that we needed.

We had to produce a pantomime that the kids would love. Santa would be called on to give each child a present and in the intervals we put on shows in which various artists would appear. We had the Daleks from Doctor Who, Batman, the Lone Ranger and on and on we went.

My great friend Wack of the *Daily Mirror* was a cartoonist whose real name was Hugh Moran. He lived in Mill Hill and did a lot of work with us for charity. He used to do sketches of the children. He also helped to relieve the pain and suffering of so many children and it was lovely to see the pain on a child's face give way to the happiest beaming smile of enjoyment. For a couple of hours the children were able to forget their troubles. Hugh Moran helped us raise thousands of pounds, he knew how to prise money out of people's pockets and he worked hard before he died. The much-needed money was for wheelchairs, special coaches and hospital equipment to make peoples lives just a bit more comfortable. The charity is still going strong, but Hugh is sadly missed.

My outside interests were with the Climbing and Hill Walking Club, to which my sons belonged. At the start I was needed as an extra driver and my wife was asked to join us as a cook (and bottle washer) – not really, we all took our turn at washing up and cooking.

We walked the Sussex and Surrey Downs every winter, come rain or shine. We also walked the Pennine Chain where we climbed Kinder Scout, Barber Booth, Feather Bed Top and many more climbs. Howden Moors, Bradfield Moors, Doctor Gate and Bleaklow Hill to Edale Cross and back to Kinder Rest were also walked by our gang. We climbed up Helvellyn in the Lake District (this mountain is 3118 feet high), Scafell Pike (3162 feet) and High Style (2644 feet), Red Pike, Rydale Fell, High Street, Beeda Fell, Old Man of Conniston; Great Gable and many other mountains were conquered by us.

But the real climbing – with these parties of underprivileged children – was in Snowdonia: on all sides of Snowdon (3559 feet), the Devils' Kitchen and the like. We climbed Glyder Fawr (3279 feet) and walked many highways and byways in Snowdonia, the Peak District, the Lake District and the Black Mountains.

We raised money in much the same way as we did in other charities and bought all the required equipment until we had thousands of pounds worth of gear. We were given a lot of equipment from Chris Bonnington's Everest expedition and the Point Five Company from Nottingham. All this made dozens of boys very happy. These lads ring me now and again and we meet for a meal or a drink; they are all now around 45 years of age. Some joined the police, one is now a sergeant, some are firemen, and most are public servants of one sort or another. All are working in their own way to help mankind and not one of them has a police record, I'm very proud to say.

We had many laughs on our journeys and expeditions and one sticks in my mind. We all went for a meal in a local pub one evening and ordered some food. The pub was packed to overflowing and when a meal was brought out by the landlady who asked whose it was, Jimmy Childe shouted to me, 'It's your meal, Jim,' so the landlady placed the meal in front of me. As she did so, a man built like a mountain came over and grunted, 'Wait your turn, that's my meal' and took it. The whole gang laughed because they had known it was his. Although I nearly got thumped, I could see the funny side of it.

Not to be outdone, on the last day of our trip, we all went shopping but Jimmy Childe wanted to be dropped off in the village of Glenridding. There were crowds around at the time and I stopped the 12-seater van. He slid back the door and the rest of the gang pushed him out of the van onto the pavement. Jimmy got up off the pathway laughing and started to run away. As he did so, I yelled out of the window, as loudly as I could, 'Stop thief'. As we disappeared up the road, we saw him being stopped by a group of people. I thought to myself, 'Get out of that one, Jimmy'.

With his gift of the gab it did not take him long.

When we returned from these trips, I was the muggins who had to carry out the repairs, do the mending and re-proofing of the tents. I also had to dry them out and store them away. Sometimes I stayed up until very late just sewing up holes in the tents, scrubbing pots and pans, until all the gear was absolutely pristine and ready to be used on the next camping trip.

Personal equipment was always checked thoroughly before any lad could even consider climbing. If we were ever to find ourselves stranded high up on a mountain, then we had to be ready with a survival kit. We made sure that all the participants had whistles, first aid, spare woollen socks, spare jumpers, waterproofs etc – just in case. In my rucksack I carried the ropes. Every day before a climb we checked and re-checked every item. The lads may have thought at the time that we were going over the top, but I can say with great pride that we never had one accident.

We went out into the snow and frost, so gloves and boots were cleaned and greased, to keep them waterproofed. There were often some lazy devils in the party, but they were made to toe the line. You couldn't risk the life of another through laziness.

I remember one morning waking up early and pulling on some clothes and making my way out of the tent. To my surprise, there was a sheet of ice (half an inch thick) off the top of the tent. It ended up in someone else's tent, which certainly made that boy get out of bed that morning.

The CID side of my life brought much contentment as we outwitted the criminals. Although I found it tiring I loved the workload and in fact I loved everything about the police force. The only unfortunate thing about my job was that I was basically spending all my time at work with little or no time for my family. The other fly in the ointment was my disillusionment with some senior officers. My wife's promotion at British Airways meant that she too was away from home for eleven hours daily.

With both sons working, one at British Airways and the other training to be an accountant, I thought that the time had come for a change in our life. We jointly decided that I should revert to being a uniformed police officer again. I realised that I would be far happier back in uniform.

I was posted to Mill Hill Police Station and was thrilled to find that my great friend, Mick Jones, was still there. When I returned to uniform, I reverted to working eight hours daily. Not only was I able to get home in time for dinner (which was something I hadn't been able to do for years), I was actually able to prepare it. I was also able to pick up my family from the local tube station and help out with any errands that needed doing. At last we could sit down as a family and have our dinner together. It had certainly been a long time since we had done that.

On my first day back at Mill Hill I was posted to late turn duty. This Police Station was only a wooden hut in those days, so every evening during late duty I would come in for my usual cup of tea.

One night as we stood drinking our tea we heard an almighty crash coming from the room we had just vacated. We rushed back and saw that a car had come right through it and into the front office. There was timber, glass and rubbish everywhere. In the middle of the heap of twisted metal (that had not long since been a motor car) emerged a lad, who looked very familiar to me.

I later learnt that he had been arrested that day for 'taking a conveyance' and had been bailed and released. To get his revenge on the police officers who had arrested him he decided to nick another car and then proceeded to ram it into Mill Hill Police Station. Which is where we came into the story.

It dawned on us that just two minutes earlier we had been standing where his car had come to a halt and it sent shivers up our spines. There had been six coppers on the very spot where the car now stood. Our senior officers were informed of what had happened and when they realised how much they might have to pay out in compensation, they decided (very quickly) to put up concrete pillars, to keep out any unwanted visitors.

Actually if you think about it, for as long as anyone can remember, prisoners have been digging holes, sawing through irons bars, even conning their way out of their cells – but this must have been the first time that someone had tried to smash *into* the police cells. The mind simply boggles.I soon got into the swing of things. When a trip to

Brighton Races came up my name was first on the list. Although Mick and I didn't bother with the races we liked to go around The Lanes, the Pavilion and other places of interest in Brighton.

On this particular occasion we went on to the Pier and saw three coppers with crates of ale sitting at the far end drinking. It wasn't long before they were leaning over the rails laying groundbait for the fish.

We went walking onwards and near the train station we came upon a young girl. She was extremely pretty and innocent-looking, but to our amazement she said to us, 'Would you like a nice young girl for the afternoon?' Whereas I just looked on completely gobsmacked, Mick, with his usual quickness of mind, came back with: 'Why, do you know where to find one?' He ducked as he saw her handbag heading in the direction of his head. Mick told her that we were police officers and I have never seen a street empty so quickly. They all have their own signals, known only to them, to warn each other that police are about.

When we returned to Mill Hill that night, I saw a crowd of drunken coppers all lined up facing the hedge chanting, *'Hughie, Hughie, Hughie!'*

What a way to end a day, sick as dogs. To this day, I don't know who Hughie was!

Dr Adenauer, the German Chancellor, visited Britain and was staying with the Queen at Windsor. I was told to take eight officers to the Castle to provide additional security during Dr Adenauer's visit.

We went on parade at 10pm, remembering what the Guvnor had told us, which was, 'Don't walk on the gravel path under the Queen's window, as she has complained that she can't sleep due to the sound of number eleven boots crashing down on the ground. Also, avoid talking – in fact do not talk at all – near the windows.' Now about twenty yards from the Queen's bedroom, in one of the side gardens, was an aviary full of parrots. When we passed by on the first night we saw that they were all on their perches fast asleep. Everywhere was as still as the night.

I walked around a corner and saw PC John Laing, a Scots lad about 6 foot 6 inches tall and who must have weighed about 20 stones. He was a BIG, and I mean BIG, lad. He had been a police officer with the Glasgow Police before transferring to the Met. He was standing under the Queen's bedroom window and as I got near him I could hear him mumbling and cursing under his breath about missing his bed on such a cold night. All of a sudden, without any warning, he drew his truncheon and with all his might threw it at the parrots' cage, hitting it full in the centre. The noise was enough to raise the dead, with parrots flapping and screaming around the cage. The noise got worse and it even woke the Guvnor, 100 yards away. Well, John stood there with the biggest grin on his face, looking extremely pleased with what he had done whilst I, on the other hand, felt that this was a very good opportunity to make myself scarce.

However, Her Majesty was 'not amused' and I spent the rest of the night writing a report which I hoped would save me from being sent to the Tower.

A lot of outlying Police Stations have trouble with gypsies. If there were a few blades of grass they would camp on it for the night. We had loads of complaints from householders about these people who would call at their doors asking for water or offering to tarmac their drives, mend roofs and so on, but most of the complaints were about their ponies and traps as they were known to race each other along the main roads and block the traffic.

I had the perfect solution for ridding us of the gypsies. I would wake them up early and nick them for stealing milk churns, which they often stole and then used for storing water. None of them could prove where they got the churns from.

Now this was OK until the Guvnor called us in. He was extremely angry and said, 'What the hell are we going to do with all these milk churns?' I must admit I hadn't thought of that, so I went to an gypsy approved site allocated to them by the Council, and spoke to the head man of the fraternity. He said that he would take the churns off our hands. I noticed his ponies and traps and when I confronted him about the racing he promised not to race on the roads in future.

He then told me a story that when he was a single man he went to town to look for a wife. He found one and married her not long after. On the way home in his horse and cart the horse fell and he shouted at it, 'That's once.' Further along the road the horse fell again and he shouted, 'That's twice.' When the horse fell a third time, he got down off the cart, took his gun and shot the horse dead.

His new wife was very angry at what she had seen and said, 'That's a terrible thing to do to that poor horse, you should be ashamed of yourself.' He turned to his wife and said, 'That's once.'

I was told that I would be required for duty at the Notting Hill Carnival, the very first such Carnival to be held in London. It was to be a big day for West Indians and the descendants of West Indians living in London. It would be a reunion of their family friends and relations, but unfortunately for me, I never got to see the end of the Carnival. It happened like this:

Trouble broke out some hours into the Carnival. The Police Commander in charge of our sector had briefed us, we had eaten breakfast, and were on duty in our allotted areas. The morning passed peacefully enough, but early in the afternoon, as we were passing a cauldron of hot water from one officer to another, it was suddenly pushed over – deliberately – and some officers received scalds requiring hospital treatment. Soon, all hell broke loose; windows were being smashed, shops were looted and damaged, and people were being assaulted by some vicious thugs who had come to watch the Carnival. We were out in force, but fighting a losing battle and were unable to contain the riot.

As I remember it, we stood with our backs to a wall while bricks and stones were hurled at us from all directions. Many officers were hit and felled in the first barrage. The officer on my right went down with a thud, blood spurting from his ear. As I knelt beside him to stop the flow of blood, I felt a number of blows to my body but they didn't hurt too much at the time.

As ambulances came to collect the injured, the rioters did everything in their power to prevent them leaving, until John Bell, a 6-foot 4-inch tall Inspector, came and took charge, with orders to clear a path to take the injured away. Then it was back to the affray. By now, the crowd was becoming more aggressive and turning their attention to some other policemen. I drew my truncheon and shouted, 'Charge!' and we chased the yobs out of the way, right to the bottom of the street. When I got to the end of the street, I looked to my left – no officers in sight. I looked to my right – no officers in sight. To the front and rear I could only see rioters converging on me, until I was completely encircled by them.

I quickly said a prayer as they got closer and closer. I was knocked to the ground by their flying fists and as I was going down, I felt many blows to all parts of my body, thudding and thudding into the soft areas of my stomach, until I passed out. I came to in the Royal Free Hospital, my wife and doctors at my side. I couldn't move and slipped in and out of consciousness.

Apparently, I was haemorrhaging badly, injured also in the shoulder, legs and both hips. I was in hospital for ten days, then sent back for physiotherapy and convalescence, before returning to Mill Hill Police Station for light duties.

One evening, three months later, I found myself driving the patrol car. The following morning I was due to have my final doctor's check-up for the all-clear. But fate had decreed that I was never to recover my health again – because it was that night that I was to receive my final injury, on duty on 28 November 1978. It was a date which I and my family – especially my wife – have never been able to forget.

Chapter Nineteen

NIL BY MOUTH

There I was in hospital waiting for my operation when early one morning I saw the familiar sign above my head 'Nil by mouth'. I was first reserve in a queue to be operated on so I didn't have to wait too long before going through the same procedure as before, needle in the bum and needle in the hand. When I woke up I was in the Intensive Care Unit where I was kept for four or five days. A number of bones had been removed and now I had the use of my back and one leg, and my body was working properly. A doctor examined me and he told me that my left leg would be paralysed forever.

I was soon up and about with the help of Mrs Israel, but this came to an abrupt end and back I went to the operating theatre. The surgeons had unfortunately left a piece of surgical equipment inside my body! After the third operation, I did some exercises and was soon walking with the aid of a frame. I was encased in a steel corset and a steel bar had been inserted down my spine. Nevertheless I was determined that as soon as I was able I would leave that hospital for rehabilitation.

My first port of call was Hendon Hospital and then I was transferred to Brighton Police Convalescent Home. By now it was March 1981 and I had spent nearly three years in hospital. Unfortunately, I was sent back to hospital again when I developed a condition called foot-drop, that is, not being able to control the foot. As I was crossing the road my foot 'flopped' out of control and I fell over. The accident left me with another injury – a bone sticking out through the skin of my elbow! However, I was soon patched up and sent back home.

I was summoned to the Police Surgeon, who showed me the hospital report, which was not too good. It ended with, *'This man will never walk again.'* He told me that as my disability was permanent, I would have to leave the Police Service and be given an 80% disability pension. There was no one else around and it was the lowest time of my life. My face must have described my feelings. The administrative staff worked out my dues and then an officer took me home without saying a word to me. I didn't say anything either, which was most unlike me, but I couldn't trust myself to say a single word.

The next thing that happened was extremely distressing for my family and me. I was given notice to quit the police house that we were living in. To add insult to injury, I was also required to pay rent for remaining in the house after I had been medically discharged from the service. I was informed that my pension and gratuity would be withheld until I left the house.

We had nowhere else to live and no close family to move in with, so we were really facing a dilemma. I did not have enough money to buy a property; it was a vicious circle from which I could see no way out.

A couple of days later I received a telephone call from a member of staff working in Scotland Yard. He had been advised to ring me to remind me that I owed them the outstanding amount of £300 and that if I didn't pay up they would take me to court. I replied, 'Let's go to court and see what the media will do with this story.'

It was time to hand in all my uniform. When I arrived at the Police Station I found that my locker had been forced open and my uniform, helmet and other belongings had been taken. That did it. This was the very first time I had snapped, I created merry hell and left feeling very unhappy.

I agreed to pay £80 for the house and it was six months before they paid my full pension. I also agreed to pay £20 for the loss of uniform, but I know they had deducted more from my pension.

I soon forgot all my troubles and got all my mates around me again. I gave the biggest leaving party that my Station had ever seen. The drinks were on me and my wife provided the food. The music was provided by one of my sons and we had a wonderful night, and all the recent bitterness was forgotten.

Later in the evening Sergeant Ken Thomas rose to his feet to make a speech in which he referred to my four Commendations. He told everyone that I was going to live in Surrey where you could hear the grass grow. To my surprise, I was showered with presents and Sergeant Thomas went on to congratulate me on raising thousands of pounds for charity over the years. He also made reference to the voluntary work that I had done for various organisations during my service.

At the close of the evening, I said goodbye to one and all and was taken home by my wife and family. I was content, but felt great sadness that I was closing the door on a big part of my life.

I went to live in Surrey, but all was not well. I was encased in plaster from my neck down to my knees. I felt completely imprisoned; I couldn't move. Back to hospital I went, but this time it was to the local hospital in Epsom before going on to Worthing Hospital, where an examination was carried out. Later I was transferred to King Edward's Hospital in Midhurst.

I was x-rayed for the hundredth time and transferred yet again, this time to Southfields Hospital where I was examined by a Mr Jarvis, the local surgeon, who prepared me for yet another operation. The concrete jacket was removed and I again went through the pre-op procedure that I knew so well. Whilst I was lying on a trolley outside the operating theatre out came Mr Jarvis, who had a little chat with me to calm my nerves. He cracked a few jokes before picking up my notes and saying, 'Now what's wrong with you?' I came straight back with, 'Well, if you don't bloody know, what am I doing lying here on this trolley!'

His laughter echoed around the room and he proceeded to wheel me into the theatre himself. Mr. Jarvis explained to me what he was going to do and showed me all the instruments he would be using. He had the most offensive weapons that I had ever seen, worse than any owned by a criminal. Luckily, I was soon off to the land of Nod.

When I came round I found I was being examined by a doctor. I asked in a very sleepy voice if everything had gone okay and he replied that it had. I asked him, 'When I get up will I be able to play the piano?' He said,

'Of course you will.' 'Well that's good,' I said, 'because I couldn't play one before!' I vaguely remember us laughing at this.

Before I left hospital all my stitches were removed, which seemed to go on forever as the wound was over twelve inches long. But I was soon my old perky self again and before long I was walking around the ward seeing what I could do to help more unfortunate patients than myself.

It wasn't long before I was allowed to go home. Sadly, gone from my life forever were my beloved pastimes of swimming, golf (I had been a four handicap), hill climbing, walking, mountaineering; all my hobbies ended on that dreadful night when I was struck down by the youth in the garage.

I have no regrets about stopping my patrol car that night and I have no hatred for the man who hit me. Funnily enough, I have never felt any hatred towards him, even though he was never brought to justice for what he did. He probably never thinks about what happened to me after he left me lying in the alley, or of the suffering that he caused my family as a result of the beating I endured, even though I now have all the time in the world to think about him.

At the time it felt as though my whole life had been snatched away from me and it took years to fully come to terms with what had happened. People often ask me now what I do with my time, knowing that the police force had been my life, but I always tell them that my days are filled with things to do.

There are many places still to explore in the world and many people to meet. I also enjoy painting. I do have my quieter moments but it is certainly wonderful to look back on the marvellous times I had in the Police Force. These are memories that I shall always treasure and no one can take them away from me.

Chapter Twenty

ENJOYING THE LAST OF THE SUMMER WINE

Twenty years since the accident, I'm enjoying life immensely. My family is a great joy to me and I now have four grandchildren, three boys and a girl. My wife Margaret and I never forget their birthdays and we always get together at Christmas. In fact, we don't need any excuse to get together. I shall never be bored, that's for sure – I think all grandparents enjoy being with their grandchildren. There are many good times to come.

We dine out whenever we can and travel throughout the UK and abroad. We especially like to visit warm countries (the sun is supposed to be good for my back) and the USA has to be a favourite country of ours. Neither my wife nor I can walk without difficulty these days; my left leg is paralysed and my back can't take too much strain. My wife has had a new knee joint and although she has made enormous strides in her recovery *(pun)* she is still unable to do very much walking. Between the pair of us, you might imagine we would be housebound but you would be so wrong. We are always on the go, out and about discovering new places of interest as well babysitting for our grandchildren.

Recently, we travelled to the USA for the winter sunshine and whilst we were there we came across an American magazine. As I began reading it I was staggered to find a photograph that had been taken in 1968 of some London policemen standing outside No.10 Downing Street guarding Harold Wilson, who was the Prime Minister at the time. They had been ordered to protect the Prime Minister against 100,000 anti-Vietnam protestors who were heading towards Downing Street. Well, I was astonished when I looked closely at the photograph to discover that my ugly mug was there amongst the cordon of police officers. I recalled the day well as the marchers, led by Tariq Ali, started their march at the Embankment and were on their way to hand in a petition to the Prime Minister to let him know that they vehemently opposed the stand that the British Government was taking on the issue.

As an aside, let me mention that during such demonstrations we often had to wait for six hours before we could take a break for refreshment, so we were always very hungry towards the end of our shift. When the protestors eventually arrived at the entrance to Downing Street, someone in the crowd threw an apple at us. Inspector John Dorking caught the apple, took a bite out of it and threw it back.

I always smile whenever I remember this story.

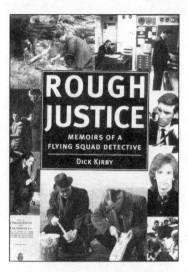